Buildings
and Memorials
of the
Channel Islands

Buildings
and Memorials
of the
Channel Islands

Raoul Lemprière

Robert Hale Limited

London

Robert Hale Limited
Clerkenwell House
Clerkenwell Green
London EC1

To

Brigadier W.D. Anderton, M.C., M.B.,

President of The National Trust for Jersey 1962–71

and

Mrs M.A. Anderton

Member of the Council of The National Trust for Jersey
1959–77

Photoset, printed and bound
in Great Britain by
REDWOOD BURN LIMITED
Trowbridge & Esher

Contents

Acknowledgements

I am indebted to the following for advice and help in the preparation of this book:

Jersey: Mr G. St C. Cornwall, Mr D.J. Cottrill, Archivist of Victoria College, Mr Robin Cox, The Reverend B.J. Giles, Rector of St Peter, The Reverend W.N. Hall, Vicar of St Mark's, The Reverend Michael Halliwell, Rector of St Brelade, Mr T.G. Hutt, The Reverend H.M. Le Feuvre, Rector of St Lawrence, Mr P. Malet de Carteret, Mr T.F. Mallet, Verger of St Helier's Church, Mr R.H. Mayne, Mr G.R. Morley, Archivist of the Jersey Methodist Circuit, Mr H.T. Porter, Mr L.P. Sinel, a Churchwarden of St Helier's Church and a Trustee of the Town Vingtaine, and Mrs Joan Stevens.

Guernsey: The Reverend A.A.E. Binns, Rector of Torteval, The Reverend K.C. Cadman, Rector of St Peter-in-the-Wood, Canon V.J. Collas, Rector of St Andrew's, The Reverend Frank Cooper, Rector of St Saviour's, Miss M.E. de Putron, The Reverend J.R. Hancock, formerly Rector of the Vale, The Reverend M.C. Millard, Rector of St Sampson's, The Reverend R.G. Nelson, Rector of Castel, Professor C. Northcote Parkinson, The Reverend J.R.A. Shaw, Rector of Forest, The Reverend Marc Trickey, Rector of St Martin's, and Lt.-Col. P.A. Wootton.

I would thank my wife for her encouragement throughout the writing of this book and especially for typing the manuscript and helping to check the proofs.

I am obliged to all those who have given permission for their photographs to be reproduced: La Société Jersiaise – the Roman Pillar at St Lawrence's Church, Jersey; *Jersey Evening Post* – Almorah Crescent, St Helier, Jersey; Lynn Photographers Limited – Mural Memorial in St Helier's Church; Mr C.R. Le Clercq – the Fonts of St Clement's Church, Grouville Church and St Matthew's Church, Lillie Langtry's Memorial, Archirondel Tower, Old Library and Greenhill, all in Jersey; Mr D.A. Fry – Music School, Victoria College, and Quetivel Mill, Jersey; Miss Marie Toms – Celtic Cross, Guernsey; Mr G.D. Lawson – Les Mouriaux House, Alderney; Mr C.W. Partridge – St Anne's Church, Alderney; Mr Carel Toms – the remainder of the photographs other than that of the unveiling of the Don Monument, St Helier, in 1885 which is from my own collection.

I am particularly obliged to Mr Toms and Mr Le Clercq for the considerable trouble they took in helping me to assemble such an interesting collection of photographs.

RAOUL LEMPRIÈRE

St Helier
13th December 1979

Illustrations

Preface

The Channel Islands, situated off the west coast of Normandy, are divided into the two Bailiwicks of Jersey and Guernsey, the former comprising Jersey and two groups of islets, Les Ecréhous and Les Minquiers, and the latter comprising Guernsey, Alderney, Sark, Herm and Jethou. The islands, including both Jersey and Guernsey despite their high density of population, retain a great deal of natural beauty. Their coastal scenery is particularly attractive and they possess long stretches of fine cliffs and numerous sandy beaches. They have miles of cliff-paths providing extensive views of the sea, the neighbouring islands and the coast of Normandy. They have pretty valleys and many miles of narrow winding lanes with old French names and bordered by small fields. Especially in springtime, the wild flowers are very beautiful, particularly in Sark and Herm and on the cliffs in Guernsey. Always present is the sea with all its varying moods and ever changing range of colours – black, grey, dark green, light green, pale blue, deep blue, the brilliant blue of a summer's day and every shade between. The sun is often shining, resulting in the islands being high in the sunshine charts, and even in winter their climate tends to be somewhat milder than that of the United Kingdom.

The Channel Islands formed part of Gaul, and when that great province, later to become France, was subjugated by the Roman legions, the islands too became part of the Roman Empire. The evidence would seem to indicate that there was no regular Roman occupation, although Roman coins and other traces of the Romans have from time to time been found. Long after the Romans had left Gaul, about 867 or possibly some years earlier, the islands almost certainly formed part of the Breton Kingdom. Some time between 933 and about 1000 they became part of the Duchy of Normandy and since 1066 when Duke William II became King William I of England, except for a few short breaks, they have been associated with the Crown of England. Since 1204, when King John lost continental Normandy, the islands have followed the fortunes of England (later Great Britain) and the islanders have been constant in their loyalty to the Crown, at the same time enjoying a large measure of self-government.

Until the beginning of the nineteenth century the inhabitants of the Channel Islands were predominantly, although not exclusively, of Norman descent as they had been when the islands formed part of the Duchy of Normandy before 1204. Until the present century those from outside the islands who down the centuries had settled there were largely assimilated into the local population. However, in more recent times the number of newcomers has been so great that they have not been absorbed, and with inevitable intermarriage between native islanders and immigrants, coupled with rapid changes in the traditional way of life, based principally on farming, the local characteristics of the people are fast disappearing.

The Channel Islands are celebrated for their cattle, 'jerseys' and 'guernseys', generous producers of high quality milk which is made into rich cream and deep yellow butter. They are also known for their woollen 'jerseys' and 'guernseys', still being made in the traditional dark blue as well as in other colours. The islands are also known for their agricultural and horticultural produce, principally early potatoes and broccoli from Jersey and tomatoes and flowers from Jersey and Guernsey. The latter island also grows splendid grapes, although, unfortunately, not as many as in time past. The islands are justly popular as holiday resorts and attract large numbers of visitors from the United Kingdom, the Continent and elsewhere; they are equally popular as tax havens for wealthy refugees. In recent years they have also become recognized financial centres as is clearly apparent from the numerous banking houses whose premises are to be seen in St Helier, the capital of Jersey, and St Peter Port, the capital of Guernsey.

Buildings are an important element in the landscape. According to their design and the materials with which they are built, so one part of a country may be distinguished from another. Even in a comparatively small country like England, the traditional buildings of one district, such as the Cotswolds, are different from those of another, such as East Anglia. These variations lend interest and variety to the scene but, unfortunately, as each year passes buildings are generally becoming more and more standardized, and one town becomes increasingly like another. The Channel Islands are no exception to the rule. Their traditional buildings, principally, but not exclusively, farmhouses, are different from those found in England and those of Jersey differ from those of Guernsey.

The buildings of the Channel Islands may be divided into a number of categories namely: ecclesiastical, military, domestic, public, commercial and miscellaneous. This last category contains a wide variety of structures, ranging from dovecots to lighthouses, from manorial court-houses to prisons. Discounting prehistoric structures, such as La Hougue Bie, Grouville, Jersey, the group with the oldest buildings is the 'ecclesiastical' containing twenty-one ancient parish churches and thirteen ancient chapels.

Jersey and Guernsey have been divided respectively into twelve and ten parishes for over a thousand years. Owing to the lack of documentary evidence, it is impossible to assess how ancient these divisions are. The opinion has been expressed that the five central parishes of Jersey – St Saviour, St John, St Mary, St Peter and St Lawrence – date from around 475. Physical evidence would appear to indicate that a church or chapel existed on the site of St Lawrence's Church, Jersey, as long ago as possibly the beginning of the seventh century. Similar evidence would indicate that a church or chapel existed on the site of Vale Church, Guernsey, as early as the seventh or eighth century. In this context it must also be borne in mind that in nearby Coutances a bishopric was certainly in being in the sixth century; that St Sampson (died about 565) is reputed to have introduced Christianity into Guernsey; that St Maglorius (died about 586), a kinsman of St Sampson, established a monastery in Sark in the same century; that excavations on the Ile Agois, an islet standing off the west side of Le Col de la Rocque, St Mary, Jersey, indicate that it could be an eremitic site dating from 600–900; and that Geroaldus, Abbot of St Wandrille (789–807) was sent by Charlemagne to an island called Augia (possibly Jersey) near the Cotentin. Some, if not all, of the other parish churches in Jersey and Guernsey are probably nearly as ancient as St Lawrence's and the Vale, although they are undocumented until some centuries later. In 1976 a celtic cross, possibly of the eighth century, was found at La Maison d'Aval, Rue des Messuriers, St Peter's, Guernsey. The cross, consisting of a long stem with three arms developed into encircling crossets, is incised into a slab of red granite now 2 feet 4 inches long, originally possibly 3 feet to 4 feet long and about 2 feet wide. It may have marked the grave of a Christian missionary from Ireland or South Wales, where similar crosses are to be seen.

In many cases the builders of the earliest churches and chapels in the Channel Islands deliberately chose sites already sacred to the inhabitants. In Jersey it is no coincidence that a chapel, Our Lady of the Dawn, was built on the top of La Hougue Bie, undoubtedly a sacred site, or that in Guernsey, Castel Church was built where a statue menhir once stood and stands again and St Martin's Church was built where another statue menhir, 'The Grandmother of the Cemetery', has always stood. It should also be mentioned that there is a possibility that St Saviour's Church, Jersey, stands on the site of a megalithic passage grave.

No reliance may be placed on the consecration dates of Jersey's parish churches, said to be derived from *Le Livre Noir de Coutances* because, although the document itself is a register of the churches in the diocese of Coutances (in which the Channel Islands were included until 1569) drawn up by order of the bishop in 1251, the consecration dates were a later addition and are completely fictitious. Similarly, no reliance may be placed on the consecration dates of Guernsey's parish churches which appear in *La Dédicace des Eglises*, a document believed to have been written either late in the sixteenth century or early in the seventeenth century.

In Jersey and Guernsey each parish church started as a small building and was gradually enlarged as and when the need arose. This becomes clear from a study of the history and development of each church. It is said that in the case of St Clement's, Jersey, a chapel within the same churchyard was incorporated with the church to form a larger building. Occasionally an extension is dated as in the case of the south-east chapel of St Mary's, Jersey, which bears the date 1342, and that of the south transept of St Peter Port, Guernsey, which bears the date 1466. Such enlargements continued right up to the Reformation by which time, with a few exceptions, the parish churches had reached approximately their present dimensions. Exceptions in Jersey are St Mary's where the south aisle was added in 1840, St John's where the chancel aisle was added in 1853, St Ouen's where the chancel was extended during the restoration of 1860–90, St Helier's where the west end of the nave was extended and a south transept added during the restoration of 1864–68 and St Peter's where the north aisle of the nave was added in 1886.

The parish churches of Jersey and Guernsey have some general resemblance resulting from the fact that they are all built of granite, are generally stone-vaulted, have towers or spires, usually centrally placed, and developed over approximately the same period of time. After that they differ in many respects, although there are similarities between one or more churches in each island. In at least one instance a church in one island, St Brelade's, Jersey, strongly resembles one in the other, St Sampson's, Guernsey. The similarity is added to by their location close to the sea (St Sampson's was even closer to the sea before the building of the quays). In passing, it should be mentioned that the fact that they alone among the ancient parish churches are dedicated to Celtic saints suggests that they may have been founded before the Norman annexation of the islands.

At the time of the Reformation the parish churches must have been similar to other comparable churches of the Catholic world. The richness of the stained glass, statuary and other embellishments would have been commensurate with the wealth of the islands.

The Reformation came to the Channel Islands as it did to England but instead of the church in the islands following the Church of

England it adopted a Presbyterian form of church government which lasted in the case of Jersey until 1623 and in the case of Guernsey until 1663. The result of this was that the churches probably suffered worse at the hands of the reformers than otherwise they would have done. They were stripped of practically every adornment and ended up with plain whitewashed walls, large pulpits and a clutter of pews and galleries. The stone altars were removed and replaced by wooden tables, brought out only when required for the quarterly communions. A number of the old altar stones were built into Mont Orgueil Castle, Jersey. Stained glass, as might have been expected, statues and plate suffered badly. Fonts fared almost as badly and only three have survived. Piscinae were more fortunate and a number exist in both Jersey and Guernsey. All Jersey's church bells, except one in each church, were removed and sold; this was not the case in Guernsey.

It was not until the nineteenth century that a start was made on restoring the parish churches to something like what they had been before the Reformation and since then all of them, with the exception of St Philip of Torteval, Guernsey, which was demolished and replaced by a new building, and Old St Anne's, Alderney, which except for its tower, was also replaced by a new building, have been restored.

Major N.V.L. Rybot, in a report on an expedition to Les Ecréhous to examine the remains of St Mary's Priory, noted down a number of characteristics held in common by Jersey's surviving ancient chapels as follows: pebble masonry secured with shell-lime cement, pointed vaulting, heavy masonry roofs, small deeply splayed windows, flat narrow bands of masonry along the exterior side walls, flat vertical angle-buttresses of low relief, the interiors plastered with shell-lime cement, wall-paintings, a piscina in the south wall near the east end to the right of the altar.

In addition to the ancient churches and chapels, the Channel Islands possess a large number of churches and chapels dating from the late eighteenth century to the present day, including a number designed by well-known Victorian architects, including Joseph Aloysius Hansom, George Frederick Bodley, Augustus Welby Northmore Pugin, Sir Arthur Blomfield and Sir George Gilbert Scott. Two outstanding churches of the present century are St Matthew's, Jersey, noted for its Lalique glass, and the very beautiful Our Lady of the Rosary, Guernsey.

The second oldest group of buildings in the Channel Islands are fortifications built to protect the islands from invasion by the French, a matter of almost constant concern from 1204 until the defeat of Napoleon I in 1815. Like the churches, the fortifications have been added to and altered down the centuries. The principal ancient buildings in this category are undoubtedly Castle Cornet, Guernsey, and Mont Orgueil Castle, Jersey, both of which are known to have existed as early as the beginning of the thirteenth century. The largest number of old fortifications to have survived date from the Napoleonic Wars when the islands were very much at risk. It is from this period that the so-called 'martello' towers date although it will be shown later that only very few are true martello towers.

None of the islands possesses any really ancient houses, although the remains of a long house of the tenth century were found at Ruette de la Tour, Cobo, Guernsey, some years ago. It had low walls, with sweeping eaves, a roof supported by wooden posts and a fireplace. Parts of some old houses, such as St Ouen's Manor, Jersey, and Sausmarez Manor, Guernsey, are no doubt extremely ancient, but for the most part the oldest surviving houses date in a few cases possibly from the sixteenth century, but generally from the seventeenth century.

The traditional Jersey and Guernsey houses continued to be built well into the nineteenth century, but from the eighteenth century onwards other types of dwelling made their appearance. In the towns of St Helier and St Peter Port vast developments took place in the late eighteenth century and during the nineteenth century, which changed their character, particularly in the case of St Helier, and vastly increased their size.

The earliest surviving buildings in the Channel Islands are constructed of granite which is scarcely surprising considering that the islands are largely composed of that material. Granite was quarried not only in the main islands but also in the neighbouring islets such as Herm, Les Ecréhous and Les Minquiers. Granite from the Chausey Islands was particularly sought after as it was easier to work than the local product. Quarrying was carried out at innumerable spots on the principal islands and someone building a house might well quarry stone from near the building site rather than from a regular quarry. The best known quarry in Jersey was Mont Mado, St John, which was worked for some centuries. In the nineteenth century and in the early years of the present century large quarries were opened up and vast quantities of granite were exported, especially from Guernsey. The local granite varies greatly in colour, from pink verging on red, right through to grey verging on blue. Pink granite is associated more with Jersey and grey granite more with Guernsey. Mont Mado granite is pink in colour and positively glows in the sunshine like old red brick. A certain amount of Caen stone was imported into the islands, as was Swanage stone for paving.

There are a number of deposits of clay in Jersey and in the nineteenth century and the present century some of these were used for brickmaking. The names principally associated with local brickmaking were 'Champion' and 'Copp'. All the brickfields appear to have been located in either the parish of St Helier or the parish of St Saviour. At one time bricks were exported from Jersey, but today none are produced in the island.

Thatch was used as a roof covering, later to be replaced by pantiles from the Low Countries and Welsh slates. In 1683 it was ordered that all houses in the town of St Peter Port were to be roofed with slates: in 1691 the owners of houses in the towns of St Helier and St Aubin were ordered within eight years to roof their properties with slates. In both cases this was to reduce the risk of fire. The only remaining thatched house in Jersey is La Caumine, Avenue du Petit Mont, St Helier, built in 1936. The thatch is of Norfolk reed. The last thatching in Guernsey was done in 1965. During the eighteenth and nineteenth centuries mahogany was imported into the islands and was used for making doors and balustrades, as well as furniture. In the nineteenth century a wider variety of materials was used for building most of which were imported from the United Kingdom. However, one important item of equipment, the kitchen range, was manufactured in Jersey by the firm of Frs J. Grandin & Co., iron founders, of Burrard Street and Commercial Buildings.

The memorials of the Channel Islands cover a wide range, from a tower built to commemorate the visit of Queen Victoria and Prince Albert to Guernsey in 1846 to a small boulder used to mark a grave and carved with the initials and date of death of the deceased. The largest group of memorials are to be found in churches, churchyards and cemeteries throughout the islands. The oldest are the gravestones built into the outside walls of some of the ancient parish churches, such as St Lawrence's, Jersey. The vast majority of gravestones up to the eighteenth century were of granite. The quality of the carving on these old stones varied considerably. Sometimes, in addition to the inscription, a gravestone bore a coat of arms or occasionally a crudely carved face. No ancient memorial brasses survive although that there were some in Guernsey is borne out by at least two existing stone matrices and a report of one which would appear to have been destroyed. In the eighteenth and nineteenth centuries granite stones gave way to imported stones which weathered badly. Marble stones were popular towards the end of the nineteenth century and in the early years of this century. Granite re-asserted itself during the last century and has continued to be used for gravestones ever since, although nowadays it is often imported and polished. There are a few examples of elegant seventeenth-century memorials, such as that to Sir Edward de Carteret in Trinity Church, Jersey, but it was not until well into the eighteenth century that fine quality monuments made their appearance in the Channel Islands in any numbers. In St Helier's Parish Church and St Peter Port Parish Church are a number of works by such distinguished sculptors as John Bacon, R.A., J. Bacon the younger, E.H. Baily, R.A., and Sir Francis Legatt Chantrey, R.A., and in the former church there are two memorials attributed to Sir Henry Cheere who was also responsible for decorative features on the pillars at the entrance gates to Sausmarez Manor, Guernsey. It was Henry's brother, John, who was the sculptor of the statue of King George II (1751) in the Royal Square, St Helier, the oldest outdoor statue in the Channel Islands excepting of course the statue menhirs in Guernsey which do not fall into the same category.

Although there are losses from time to time, the old and historic buildings and memorials of the Channel Islands are for the most part well cared for. This has been due not only to financial prosperity in the islands since the end of World War II but also to the work of such bodies as The National Trust for Jersey (1936), The National Trust of Guernsey (1960) and the Alderney Society (1966) which has had the effect of educating the public to appreciate old and historic buildings. Even the German fortifications dating from the Occupation, once unloved, are now studied by the Channel Islands Occupation Society (1962) which publishes authoritative accounts of them from time to time. The States of Jersey and the States of Guernsey have many ancient monuments in their care and both have passed legislation designed, in the case of the former, to protect buildings of architectural and historic interest, and in the case of the latter, buildings, structures and other objects of historic, traditional, archaeological or other interest.

It is hoped that this book will help to stimulate interest still further in the insular heritage by giving the reader an idea of the many historic and beautiful buildings which the islands possess. The more that the public knows about them and their history, the more likely it is to appreciate them and to want to preserve them. So often a worthwhile building or memorial is demolished or allowed to fall into disrepair because the public does not know about it or, if it does, is ignorant of its historic and architectural interest. Despite all endeavours, there are always those who for one reason or another want to destroy something worth preserving. Constant vigilance is required by those who care. As that much respected Guernsey historian the late Edith Carey once wrote "The only enemy these old monuments have to fear is the sacrilegious hand of man".

1

The Ancient Parish Churches of Jersey

ST HELIER'S CHURCH, often referred to as the 'Town Church' as it is located in the heart of the town of St Helier, stands in a churchyard bounded on three sides by busy thoroughfares, Church Street, Mulcaster Street and Bond Street.

The church, which is known to have existed at least as early as 1066, underwent a major restoration 1864–68. It is stone-vaulted, except for the west end of the nave and the south transept, and roofed with tiles. It has a central tower built of rectangular blocks of dressed granite, with a straight parapet, pierced on all four sides by quatrefoil openings, and a stair turret. It has five gargoyles. The tower has belfry windows on the top storey on the north and south sides. It also has a clock with two faces, one on the east side and one on the west, which bears the name "John Le Gallais" and dates from 1862. The interior of the church consists of a nave with a gallery at its west end and a vestry on its north side, a south aisle, crossing, north transept, south transept with a gallery at its south end and a chancel.

The nave, extended to its present length in 1864–68, is divided from the south aisle by an arcade consisting of circular pillars with octagonal capitals. On the west wall, to the left of the door, and on the north wall, between the west and centre windows, are three oak boards on which are painted a list of all the known rectors from Nicolas du Pont (de Ponte) (1294) to the present day. On the south wall, on the west side of the gate and staircase giving access to the west gallery, is an oak board on which are painted the names of the churchwardens from 1800. In the south-west corner of the nave stands a large square granite font supported on a large central pillar and four small pillars. On the sides of the bowl are carved, one on each side, a dove, an anchor, a lamb and the sun.

There is arcading on the east and west walls of the north transept. Against the west wall stands a frontal chest, a gift from the diocese of New Jersey to mark the tercentenary of the State (1663–1963).

In the east wall of the south transept is a glass-fronted treasury (1965) in which is displayed part of the church's collection of silver. It is a memorial to Matthew Le Marinel, Dean of Jersey (1937–59). Above it is an enlarged and coloured reproduction of the design on his decanal seal. The dean's ashes are interred under the paving at the crossing, the first burial to take place in the church since 1838, and the spot is marked by a stone inscribed "Matthew Le Marinel – Priest – Rector – Dean 1963".

The church plate comprises: four cups, two presented in 1767 and two in 1777, and two flagons all made by Pierre Amiraux, a Jersey silversmith; another cup (electroplate), a paten and a wine strainer, the former bearing the London hallmark for 1824 and the latter bearing the London hallmark but with the date indistinct, both presented in 1826; a platter bearing the maker's mark "RB", presented in 1704; a baptismal dish bearing the London hallmark for 1685 and presented in 1731; a shaped circular platter with gadrooned edge, shell – and diaper-work border, engraved under the rim with three winged cherubs' heads, bearing the maker's mark "IG" (possibly Jean Gruchy of Jersey) under a crown twice in the bowl, and presented in 1740; a platter exchanged in 1799 for two cups which had become unusable; a paten bearing the London hallmark for 1904; a paten (probably electroplate), and a miniature communion set.

The church also possesses a five-lobed, wavy-edge pewter plate with gadrooned rim by Hellier Perchard. It bears the inscription "DON DE M. JEAN DE STE. CROIX A LA PAROISSE DE ST. HELIER 1744".

The church holds the communion plate of Elizabeth Castle comprising a chalice (1640), flagon (1608) and paten on foot (1621) all bearing the London hallmark, and the letters "W.D." on either side of an arrow head added about 1906. The chalice and the paten bear the arms of Sir Thomas

Jermyn, Governor of Jersey (1631–44). The flagon bears a coat of arms, probably that of Lord Capel. The set was placed in the custody of the Dean of Jersey for the use of St James's Church at garrison services.

In addition, the church is the proud custodian of a crucifix and candlesticks presented to Jersey by Queen Elizabeth, now the Queen Mother, as a thank-offering for the Liberation.

At the crossing by the south side of the chancel stands a fine brass lectern presented by Francis Bertram.

In the chancel there are clear signs of openings, now blocked up, above the arches, on the north and south sides.

A painting of *The Last Supper* serves as a reredos. It was presented by the congregation as a tribute to the memory of the Reverend Philip Alfred Lefèvre, Vice-Dean 1880–88, who died while ministering at the altar on 31 March 1889. There is a brass plate to his memory on the wall to the left of the altar. On the right of the altar is a piscina (not an original).

The screens, dividing the chancel from the chapel known as the Mortuary Chapel on its north side and the Lady Chapel on its south side, were erected by the people of Jersey in 1932 to commemorate the work of Samuel Falle who had been Dean of Jersey and Rector of St Helier since 1906. On the left of the inscription on the north screen towards its east end, are the arms of the deanery impaling those of Falle.

In passing it should be mentioned that the arms of the deanery are derived from those of Richard Mabon, Dean of Jersey for several periods between 1509–43.

The somewhat elaborate canopied dean's chair in the sanctuary was presented to the church by Dean Le Marinel in memory of his parents, Philip Le Marinel and Eva Louisa Le Marinel. The chair is partly gilded and bears the arms of Jersey quartered with the arms of the deanery. The chair next to the dean's was presented to the church by the Bishop of New Jersey to commemorate his visit to the island on 20 July 1960. The dean's stall at the west end of the chancel, south side, and the stall opposite commemorate Dean Falle, Dean and Rector 1906–37, in which latter year he died.

The Mortuary Chapel contains the organ originally built by Jardine and Company in the early 1920s and rebuilt by John

Compton Organ Company Limited in 1962. In the north wall of the chapel are two arched recesses. The Lady Chapel was furnished as such in 1952.

The church has the following stained-glass windows: north transept given by Philip Le Rossignol, "Christ Walking on the Sea"; nave: (north wall, east window), the gift of Jean de Gruchy, "The Raising of Lazarus"; (north wall centre window), the gift of Mrs M. L. Pepin in memory of her son, Arthur Reginald Pepin, "St Elizabeth and her Son, John the Baptist", 1977; (north wall, west window) presented by Mrs John Le Mesurier, "The Annunciation" by H. T. Bosdet. This window was formerly in the vestry and was re-sited in 1975; (west window), presented by George Bertram, "The Crucifixion"; (two panels in the window at the west end of the south wall) paid for by subscription among the widows of the congregation, "Christ, the Good Shepherd". These panels were formerly in the window of the Mortuary Chapel and were re-sited in 1971; south aisle: (west window), presented by the Westaway family, "The Ascension"; (south wall, west window), presented by the sons of Abraham de Gruchy, "The Baptism of our Lord"; (centre window), given by N. Le Quesne, "Christ Blessing the Children"; (south wall, east window), presented by Jurat J. G. Falle, the subjects represented being "The Healing of the Woman", "Christ, the Consoler", and "St Peter Walking on the Sea"; south transept: (south window) given by the parish of St Helier, "The Sacrifice of Isaac", "The Framing of the Law", and "The Brazen Serpent"; (east window), the coats of arms of King Charles II and Queen Elizabeth the Queen Mother, both of whom attended service in the church; Lady Chapel: (west window), given by François Le Breton in memory of members of the Le Breton family; the subjects of the three panels being "Christ appearing to St Thomas", "St Paul preaching at Athens" and "The Woman of Samaria". The brass plate beneath the window records the names of those remembered and bears the Le Breton Arms at its centre; (east window, south side), the gift of Jurat E. C. Malet de Carteret, the subject being "Christ Healing the Sick". On a brass plate beneath this window is an inscription, with the de Carteret

Arms beneath, which if glanced at cursorily makes the reader raise his eyebrows, it runs as follows:

> To the Glory of God and in Memory of George Frederick de Carteret his Cousin who perished by drowning and lies interred in the Cathedral Church Galway Ireland this window is given by Edward Charles Malet de Carteret Seigneur de St. Ouen A.D. MDCCCLXVI

In fact de Carteret, an ensign in the 30th Regiment, was not buried in Galway Cathedral but at St Nicholas Church, Galway City, where there is a mural memorial in the church to his memory and that of his wife Elizabeth, who was also a native of Jersey, which records that he died by drowning when he fell into the docks; (east window), given by the Restoration Committee, four lights, representing "The Adoration of the Magi", "Christ in the Temple", "The Marriage Feast in Cana" and "Christ Bearing His Cross"; chancel, (east window), the gift of the Hemery family. The upper section represents "The Lord Enthroned" and the lower sections represent "The Angel Announcing the Resurrection" and "The Risen Lord Appearing to Mary Magdalene". This window was the work of one of the most eminent artists of the period, and was exhibited at the Great Exhibition of 1862, as an example of British ecclesiastical art.

The church contains a number of interesting memorials. Among those commemorated are: nave, north side, west to east – Jean Le Capelain (1812–48), artist, sometimes called the 'Jersey Turner' – granite memorial (1948 – erected by La Société Jersiaise); Major and Brevet Lieutenant-Colonel Philip Walter Jules Le Gallais (died 1900) – marble memorial above north door (1900 – erected by the States of Jersey); Alfred Charles Le Quesne, Brevet Major, Bengal Staff Corps, 5th Regiment of Infantry, Hyderabad Contingent, who died of cholera at Jhelum, Punjaab, – marble memorial; Magnus Kempenfelt, Lieutenant-Governor (died 1727); Clement John de Quetteville (died 1835) and Esther Elizabeth de Quetteville (née Nicolle), his wife (died 1876); Michel Lemprière (1606–71), Parliamentary Bailiff – granite memorial (1917 – erected at the instance of R. R. Lemprière, Lord of the Manor of Rozel): north transept, west side – J. Lamb, Captain in the 35th Regiment and Assistant Barrack Master General (died 1795) – marble memorial with arms at head; Charles d'Auvergne (died 1797) (1799 – erected by his second surviving son Philip, Duke of Bouillon) and Elizabeth d'Auvergne (née Bandinel), wife of Charles d'Auvergne (died 1803) (inscription added by her daughter, Ann Le Gros); north side – Jean Hue (died 1807) and Jean Hue, his eldest son, Lieutenant in the 2nd Regiment of Guards (died 1803); John La Cloche, Rector of Trinity (died 1811), and Esther La Cloche (née Patriarche), his wife (died 1801), and other members of the family; William Claude Hamilton (died 1859), Edouard Patriarche (died 1697) and others – marble memorial: Lady Chapel, north-east wall – Lieutenant-General Andrew Gordon, Lieutenant-Governor (died 1806) – marble memorial; Philip Filleul (died 1875) and Catherine Elizabeth Blanche Filleul (née Valpy), his wife (died 1873) – marble memorial; east wall – granite memorial to those who fell in World War I; south wall – Major Francis Peirson, hero of Battle of Jersey (died 1781) (1784 – by John Bacon, R. A.) – a marble memorial, commissioned by the States at a cost of 300 guineas. There is also a stone let into the paving at the crossing, inscribed "PEIRSON" which marks the hero's resting-place. Magdalene de Carteret (née Durell), widow of Sir Edward de Carteret (died 1743) – elaborate marble memorial (after October 1747 – attributed to Sir Henry Cheere). The inscription, in the most flattering terms, reads as follows:

> Near this place is deposited the body of Dame Magdalene Durell, relict of Sir Edward de Carteret, Knt., daughter of John Durell Esq, Lieut.-bailiff & jurat of the Royal Court of this island by Ann Dumaresq, his wife.
> In the person of this Lady, most beloved, when alive, most lamented, when dead, were displayed every Christian grace, every natural & acquired ornament that can recommend or entitle the possessor to the favor of God and man. For piety, a saint; for charity, a parent to the poor; for meekness, modesty & patience, temper'd with affability & cheerfulness, an example to be imitated by all, exceeded by none. That God would graciously be pleased to bless the world with characters of this sort should be the prayer of every one, who is a friend to

human-kind. She died June 12. 1743, aged 69.

The brave but unfortunate Philip de Sausmarez Esq, (son of Matthew de Sausmarez of the island of Guernsey by Anne Durell, his wife) Commander of his Majesty's ship Nottingham, who acquired glory to his country by his death, being slain in the sea fight, when the French were defeated on the 14th of October 1747, ordered this monument to be raised in memory of this lady, his aunt, from a love of her virtues, gratitude for favors, & sorrow for her death.

There is a monument to Philip de Sausmarez by Sir Henry Cheere in Westminster Abbey, South aisle: Brigadier Thomas John Anquetil (died 1842) who was killed in command of the British and Bengal troops whilst fighting hand to hand with the enemy near Jugdulluk in the Cabool passes; Corbet Hue, Rector and Dean, (1838), Major-General Archibald Campbell, Lieutenant-Governor (died 1838) and Martha Elizabeth Campbell, his wife (died in London 1868). There is also a stone bearing an inscription let into the paving at the crossing which marks his resting-place. John Durell, King's Advocate (died 1725), Elizabeth, his wife (died 1724) and Captain George Durell, R.N., their son (1754) (after May 1754 – attributed to Sir Henry Cheere) – elaborate marble memorial featuring an urn, flanked on either side by a portrait bust, and three cherubs heads with wings at the base; Philip John Ouless (1817–85), marine and landscape painter – granite memorial (1972 – erected by some of his descendants). On the west wall of the south aisle are three memorials. The first is a marble tablet to Thomas Adderson (died 1923) – "Headmaster of the National School in this Parish" for thirty-seven years (1884–1921), subscribed for by his 'Old Boys'. The second, the oldest in the church, is of Caen stone and is to Maximilian Norreys who died in 1591 while serving with the army of Henry IV, King of France and Navarre. The third is of slate to Garthruda Amy, wife of Captain Thomas Amy (died 1647). On it are carved the arms of Amy (of Cornwall) impaling those of Enysea.

In the church are preserved the colours of the Fourth or South Regiment (St Helier Battalion) laid up in 1878. The colours hang from the east face of the south-west pillar of the crossing. In the church are also preserved the colours of the Third or South Regiment, presented in 1879 and laid up in 1925, and those of the Royal Jersey Militia, presented by the States and laid up in 1954. The former are displayed in two glass-fronted frames attached to the front of the south gallery and the latter in two glass-fronted frames attached to the front of the west gallery. On the wall to the left of the staircase giving access to that gallery is part of the colours of the Royal Jersey Artillery, St Helier Section, of 1827, presented to Colonel H. M. Vatcher, M.C., and officers of the Royal Jersey Militia Mess by R. C. Robin, Coldstream Guards in 1935.

The church has two bells, one dated 1633, cast by M. C. Picard and the other dated 1847, cast by C. & G. Mears of London.

The parish registers are preserved as follows: baptisms from 1596; marriages and deaths from 1663.

There is a statue of St Helier above the north door.

Let into the ground at the base of the exterior walls of the church are a number of gravestones including: north side, in line with the north transept: west, pink granite stone bearing the date "1657" and the initials "M.D.": east, a rather battered pink granite stone crudely carved with an inscription to the memory of Thomas En?ey and Rachel Parker, his wife (died 1742): west side, north to south: grey granite stone in memory of Philip Durell, Junior, who died on 31st [*sic*] April 1755 aged four years and eight months and Anne Le Vavasseur-dit-Durell (died 1822); pink granite stone in memory of a refugee, almost certainly a Huguenot who sought refuge in Jersey following the revocation of the Edict of Nantes and died in the island in 1690; pink granite stone in memory of Abraham Le Vavasseur-dit-Durel (died 1665).

Standing against the southern exterior of the Lady Chapel are two gravestones commemorating French royalists who died in Jersey. The one closer to Church Street commemorates Dame Charlotte Françoise Marie Reine de Coëtlogon wife of Messire Marie Jacques du Bahuno, Marquis du Liscoët, a French royalist refugee (died 1791) – soft stone with arms at head. The inscription on the other is no longer legible.

In the churchyard there are also to be seen memorials to: Jean Laffoley died in 1759 aged 100 years and 4 months and to Richard Henly (died 1821) and Henrietta A. F. Henly (née March), his widow (died 1852) – with arms at head as well as several small rectangular granite memorials, inscribed only with the deceased's initials and the year of death, in the south-west angle of the church. There is also a small rectangular granite stone inscribed "Rullecourt 6 Janvier 1781", commemorating Philippe Charles Félix Macquart, Baron de Rullecourt, who commanded the French at the Battle of Jersey and was killed during the fighting, let into the grass immediately opposite the west door.

Near the south-west corner of the churchyard is a plain octagonal bowl of Chausey granite with an outlet hole which has been blocked up.

Along the north side of the churchyard is a block of buildings comprising Church House (west end) and Norwich Union House (east end) (1970 – by Taylor Leapingwell). In Church House the window on the staircase giving access to the first floor is filled with granite tracery. The paving to the south and west of the building is composed of old gravestones.

The churchyard is bounded by a granite wall surmounted by iron railings made by Joseph Le Rossignol in 1845 to a design by Jean Le Capelain, possibly the artist. There is a gateway giving access from Church Street on the east and another giving access to Bond Street on the west. Let into the outer side of the wall to the left of the former is the poor-box bearing on its front the quotation "*Celui qui a pitié du pauvre prête à l'Eternel, et il lui rendra son bien fait*" (He that hath pity upon the poor lendeth unto the LORD; and that which he hath given will he pay him again – Proverbs Chapter 19, Verse 17). Poor-boxes such as this are a feature of the ancient parish churches. The iron screen in the opening in the Bond Street wall, towards the Broad Street end, came from the chapel of the prison which once stood at the corner of Gloucester Street and Newgate Street and bears a small plaque to that effect.

The pavement bordering the churchyard on its Church

Street and Mulcaster Street sides is paved with rectangular
stones, each the width of the pavement, to mark the area of
the churchyard which was incorporated in the two thoroughfares when they were widened pursuant to an Act of the States
of 1844. The Act provides that the parish shall pay the sum of
five shillings a year to the rector for the use of the land included in the enlargement of the two roads.

The building on the east side of Bond Street (La Rue de la
Madelaine) adjoining the churchyard stands on the site of the
Chapel of the Madelaine.

GROUVILLE CHURCH (St Martin of Grouville) is situated on
a corner site on the north side of Rue à Don. There is an
extension to the churchyard on the opposite side of the road.

The church, which is known to have existed at least as early
as 1066, is stone-vaulted and roofed with slates. It has a
central belfry and spire (Le Pointu de Grouville), rendered in
cement in 1788, surmounted by a weathercock, and with a
string course near the top and long narrow slits at the base for
light. In the belfry is a clock with two faces, one on the east
side and one on the west. The interior of the church consists
of a nave (the oldest part of the building) and a chancel with a
chapel on either side. The north chapel, La Chapelle des
Amis, has been divided into two. The east end serves as a
Lady Chapel and the west end as a vestry. The windows vary
greatly in size and style. One on the north side of the nave,
towards the west end, is long and narrow and almost certainly
formed part of the original building from which the present
nave has developed.

In the south-west corner of the nave stands the font of
Chausey granite which is a rarity as it contains a subsidiary
basin within the main one. The font was given to the church
by La Société Jersiaise which became its owner when it purchased La Hougue Bie. The font probably came originally
from St Helier's parish church from which it was removed at
the Reformation. Subsequently it was taken to La Hougue
Bie. The oak cover dates from 1935.

On the south wall of the nave is an oak board on which is
painted a list of all the known rectors from early times to the

present day, starting with Pierre Falaise (?–1309–15).

Above the chancel arch are the Royal Arms. On the right of the altar in the chancel is a piscina; there is another in La Chapelle des Amis.

In the south chapel is a recess, almost at floor level, which would have been approximately two feet above the floor before the latter was raised in 1838. Within the recess is a curious carved head with a hole in the middle of its forehead. There were traces of wall-paintings in the chapel.

On the south-east corner of the crossing, standing on a granite pillar, is a granite bowl, probably dating from the fourteenth or fifteenth century, carved with a monogram, possibly "S.M.", and an elaborate design. The outlet is in the shape of a heart. The bowl was mounted on the pillar in 1978 as a memorial to Edgar Aleck Dorey, C.B.E., and Olive Dorey (née Giffard), his wife, former residents of the parish.

Most of the windows in the church are filled with stained glass including: chancel, east window, depicts "Scenes of the Passion"; La Chapelle des Amis, east window (1873), depicts "Incidents in the Life of St Martin of Tours" with the arms of the donor, Frederick Shirley de Carteret Bisson, and of the family of Dumaresq du Morin beneath. The window was designed by J. B. P. Payne and beside it, affixed to the wall, is a model of the window at the base of which is a brass plate stating that the window was designed by the author of *An Armorial of Jersey*; south chapel, east window, depicts "The Four Evangelists"; other windows depict "The Good Shepherd", "Nativity" and "Pentecost".

Among the memorials in the church is one to Sir Herbert Lunsford, Lieutenant-Governor from 1675 until his death at Gorey Castle in 1680. It is located almost opposite the font, and bears his arms. On the wall of the vestry is an oval marble memorial to John Williams and Mary Williams, his wife, who died respectively in 1786 and 1783. On the south wall of the south chapel is a marble memorial with Latin inscription, surmounted by the arms of Payn, to the memory of Francis Payn, Dean of Jersey (1729–75).

Hanging at the west end of the nave, on the north side, is the standard of the original Jersey Overseas Contingent Association D Company 7th Battalion Royal Irish Rifles placed in the safekeeping of the church in memory of the 304 officers, N.C.O.s and men of the Royal Jersey Militia who volunteered for service overseas under the command of Major W. A. Stocker in World War I.

The church plate includes: four cups, a two-handled bowl (probably electroplate), a ewer by Jacques Quesnel a Jersey silversmith, two platters, a baptismal dish, also by Quesnel, a cup, flagon and paten (1854), a paten on foot (1886), a paten (mounted shell) (1903). A treasury is to be installed shortly.

The church also has two collecting pots each dated on the base "1750" and inscribed "*Paroisse de Groville* [sic] *1750*".

In the tower is a bell originally cast in London in 1768 and refounded in Villedieu in 1881. It bears the names of the rectors, churchwardens and parish trustees at the time of the casting and re-founding and the inscription "Let everything that hath breath, praise the Lord, praise the Lord" (original in French).

The church registers are preserved from 1584 although they contain some gaps.

Exterior features of the building worth noting are: two gargoyles, one on either side of the west gable of the chancel; part of an ancient gravestone built into the southern buttress of the east wall of the chancel; nearby part of what is believed to have been a representation of the arms of the Mallet family.

In the churchyard is a memorial to soldiers of the 83rd Regiment killed by the French at Platte Rocque on 6 January 1781.

The poor-box is let into the exterior wall of the churchyard to the right of the south gateway.

The rectory stands on the north side of the churchyard and the parish hall, formerly Grouville Central School (1855–56), is a short distance away near the foot of Grouville Hill.

ST BRELADE'S CHURCH is situated by the sea at the west end of St Brelade's Bay. The churchyard is bordered on the east by the slipway and the sea-wall, on the north by Mont Sohier, on the west by a road and on the south by the rectory garden. The church's picturesque aspect and situation causes it to be in great demand for weddings.

The church, which is known to have existed at least as early as 1066, is stone-vaulted and roofed with tiles. It has a saddleback tower to which access is obtained by a circular stair turret looking like a shortened version of an Irish round tower. The interior of the building consists of a nave with a porch at its west end, nave aisle, built in 1537, crossing, transepts, chancel and St Mary's Chapel to the north of the chancel. The walls have been stripped of their plaster and consequently the church is rather dark inside. However, a splendid concealed lighting system has been installed which reveals every detail of the vaulting. In the north wall of the west porch is a recess which once held a holy water stoup.

On the west wall of the nave, immediately to the north of the west door, is a board on which is a list of all the known rectors from early times to the present day. The first on the list is Ranulphe Maret (1296–?). Between the west door and the nave aisle door is the ancient font composed of two blocks of Chausey granite, with two indentations on the rim of the bowl, and now with an oak cover. It was found in 1845 by a picnic party among the furze bushes on the hillside behind the church.

The oak pulpit has carved on it a rendering in French of Proverbs, Chapter 25, Verse 11, which in English reads "As golden apples are filligreed with silver so is the true word".

At the entrance of the chancel was a rood-loft which is evidenced by the corbels on which it rested and the doorway, now blocked up, which gave access to it. Today the chancel is divided from the nave by a carved oak screen.

The chancel is paved with granite from La Moye, L'Etacq, Plemont and Ronez. The stone altar with five consecration crosses came from Mont Orgueil Castle into whose fabric it had been built at the Reformation. On its south side is a rare double piscina which probably dates from between 1272 and 1307. One basin was used by the priest for washing his fingers before the consecration and the other for the ablutions or rinsing of the chalice.

Every principal window in the building is filled with stained glass, much of it by Bosdet. Above the nave aisle door is a window in memory of John Martell (1694–1753), a Jersey-man, who founded La Maison d'Eaux-de-Vie Martell, the famous brandy firm. The south window of the sanctuary was given in 1872 in memory of William Braithwaite.

The church contains memorials to, among others: Lieutenant-General John Le Couteur (died 1835), a dis-tinguished soldier; Mary Le Couteur (née Dumaresq), the General's widow (died 1845); Harriet Le Couteur (née Janvrin), wife of Colonel (later Sir John) Le Couteur (died 1865); Sir John Le Couteur, F.R.S. (died 1875); Anne Luce (died 1874), who was in the service of the Le Couteur family for fifty-five years; a number of memorials to members of the Pipon family.

The church plate includes: four bowls, used as communion cups, baptismal dish (1808), dish, flagon (1811), two collect-ing pots (1859), a silver cross and candlesticks, a chalice and paten. The church also owns a processional cross and three copper collecting pots inscribed "ST BRELADE 1819".

The church has one bell cast by John Warner & Sons, London, in 1883, inscribed with the names of the rector, constable, centeniers, parish trustees and the churchwardens.

The parish registers are preserved from 1560.

Exterior features of the building worth noting are the gar-goyle on the west front, cable moulding round the arch of the nave aisle door, the dripstone with a fleur-de-lis at its head over the central window on the south side of the nave and the sundial let into the gable of the south transept, dated 1837 and inscribed *"L'homme est semblable à la vanité: ses jours sont comme une ombre qui passe Ps. 144, v. 4."*.

In the churchyard there are two splendid oak trees, one to the west of the church beside the path leading from the lych-gate to the main entrance and the other to the south-west of the building.

Memorials worth noting are those to: Jean Baillehache (died 1652), taking the form of a granite chest tomb to the right of the south porch, Marie Bartlett (née Mauger), widow of Francis Bartlett, (1677–1741), who founded the General Hospital (monument erected by the States); Campbell Pater-son "Founder of Camp Coffee, Glasgow, 1888" who died in

Jersey in 1927, aged 76.

The archway giving access to the churchyard from close by the slipway dates from the enlargement of 1852 and was designed by Sir John Le Couteur. The stepped top of the archway was a subsequent addition the cost of which was met out of moneys collected by Lady Le Couteur.

The lychgate (1933) was given by Lady Trent in memory of her husband, Jesse Boot, First Baron Trent of Nottingham, the founder of Boots the chemists.

The Perquage or Sanctuary Path consists of a flight of stone steps leading from the churchyard directly to the beach.

The church hall stands on the corner across the road from the west side of the churchyard, and there is an extension to the churchyard on the opposite corner.

Beside the narrow roadway leading to Le Coleron, within a railed-off area, is the private burial-place of the Trent family. There are buried Jesse Boot, First Baron Trent of Nottingham (1850–1931), Florence Lady Trent (1863–1952) and John Campbell, the Second Baron (1889–1956).

ST CLEMENT'S CHURCH (St Clement of Pierreville), the smallest of Jersey's ancient parish churches, serves the island's smallest parish. Its churchyard is bounded on the south by St Clement's Inner Road, on the south-west by La Rue du Moulin and on the east by La Rue Laurens.

The church is stone-vaulted and roofed with slates. It has a central belfry and spire, rendered in cement, surmounted by a weathercock, and with long narrow slits at the base for light. In the southern face of the belfry is a clock, presented in 1919 in memory of David Hocquard, Rector (1804–22). Beneath the clock is a small window. The two centre windows high up in the north wall of the nave are very ancient and almost certainly formed part of the original building from which the present nave has developed. The interior of the church consists of the nave, crossing, north and south transepts, chancel and a chapel to the north of the chancel.

It is said that originally there were two chapels standing in the churchyard, now respectively the nave and the chapel to the north of the chancel. Be that as it may, an opening connecting the chapel with the north transept was made after the wall-painting on the east wall of the transept was painted as is evidenced by the fact that the centre of the painting was destroyed when the connecting arch was constructed.

The nave has a central aisle and no side aisles. On the north wall is an oak board presented in memory of William Anderton and Mary Anderton (née Dinsdale), his wife, on which is a list of all the known rectors from early times to the present day. The first on the list is Guillaume du Cotentin (?–1302). High up on the same wall, towards the east end, is a wall-painting, one of a number found in the summer of 1879 during the restoration of the church. It depicts St Michael and the dragon. Towards the west end of the south wall is a door which gives access to the former vestry.

At the corner of the nave and the south transept stands the beautiful font made of Chausey granite and dating from either the fourteenth or fifteenth century. At the Reformation it was buried in the churchyard from which it was retrieved in the middle of the nineteenth century.

Close by the north-east corner of the nave, beside the arch giving access to the crossing, and about eye level, a granite corbel protrudes from the wall, its front carved with the Payn Arms, which may not at first be apparent as the tail of one of the trefoils is missing. Before the Reformation it may have supported a statue.

The arches at the crossing are of squared granite chamfered at the corners and with chamfer stops. The ceiling of the crossing has quadrilateral stone-vaulting with ribs rising from the arches to a central circular opening beneath the belfry. There are stone seats built into the base of each side of the chancel arch.

The oak pulpit on a granite base was erected to the memory of those killed in World War I, and the wooden lectern was presented by Charles Marett, Rector (1842–76).

A glass-fronted treasury (1963) is set into the west wall of the north transept where there once was a doorway. In it is displayed the church's collection of plate which includes: six chalices, one bearing the London hallmark for 1653 and two the London hallmark for 1804, a platter, a baptismal dish, a

(*Above left*) Part of a pillar at St Lawrence's Church, Jersey, as it stood originally in the portico of a Roman villa of the third or fourth century. (*Above right*) With the flat head of its capital used for an epitaph in about A.D. 600 (*Below*) With its back decorated as an architectural ornament in the eighth or ninth century.

(*Above left*) A tombstone outside the west front of Vale Church, Guernsey, dating from the seventh or eighth century. (*Above right*) Celtic cross, possibly of the eighth century, at La Maison d'Aval, Rue des Messuriers, St Peter-in-the-Wood, Guernsey, which may have marked the grave of a Christian missionary

The chancel of Vale Church, Guernsey

Castel Church, Guernsey

St Martin's Church, Jersey

(*Above left*) Pre-Reformation font at St Brelade's Church, Jersey. (*Above right*) Pre-Reformation font at St Clement's Church, Jersey. (*Below left*) Rare pre-Reformation font with a subsidiary basin within the main one at Grouville Church, Jersey. (*Below right*) Glass font at St Matthew's Church, Jersey – the only one in the British Isles

(*Above left*) Man's head and (*above right*) woman's head carved on corbels at St Lawrence's Church, Jersey
(*Below left*) Girl's head and (*below right*) comic head carved on corbels at St Lawrence's Church, Jersey

Flamboyant south porch of St Martin's Church, Guernsey

Mural memorial attributed to Sir Henry Cheere, Bt., at St Helier's Church, Jersey

Stained-glass window by Miss M.E. de Putron at St Peter-in-the Wood Church, Guernsey, depicting St Peter wearing a guernsey

Small gravestones let into the west wall of the churchyard of St John's Church, Jersey

paten bearing the London hallmark for 1861, two alms dishes bearing the London hallmark for 1843, a wafer box and a private communion set comprising a chalice, a paten, a wafer box, a spoon and two small glass flagons for the wine and water. The church also owns two copper collecting pots, one inscribed and dated 1738.

On the east wall of the north transept (as mentioned earlier) are the two ends of a large wall-painting depicting part of St Margaret with one wing of her dragon and St Barbara holding a palm and standing beside her tower.

On the west wall of the south transept are parts of another wall-painting showing two horses' legs and two dogs' heads with a verse beneath in French which translated reads "Alas, St Mary! Who are these three corpses who look so grim? It breaks my heart to see them thus piteous". These are the remains of a painting called *The Three Living and The Three Dead* which is told in a thirteenth-century French poem, Baudoin and de Condé's *Dit des trois morts et les trois vifs*. Versions of this subject are to be found on the walls of a number of churches, including Castel Church, Guernsey. Usually three young kings or courtiers are depicted, sometimes on horseback, sometimes on foot, out hunting in the forest, enjoying the pleasures of life, when they meet three skeletons, who warn them that all must die, rich and poor, and become as they are. The painting was done before the crossing was formed as it is to-day because its south-west pillar occupies the space once occupied by the north end of the picture.

Two further wall-paintings (V and VI) mentioned in the Reverend R. Bellis's article on the wall-paintings published in 1880 have since disappeared. They were on the north-east corner of the nave on either side of the window. They depicted on the west side a woman, wearing a head-dress, surrounded by an aureole, seated on a Roman chair and the word *"Sancta"*; on the east side a woman, wearing a head-dress holding some sort of container in her right hand and lifting the lid with her left. At the side of the painting was a banderole, bearing in Gothic letters the name "Maria" followed by a longer word beginning with "M".

The chancel is divided from the chapel to the north by two arches with octagonal capitals. Within the spandrel between the two arches is a shield bearing the Payn Arms. To the right of the altar is a piscina with pointed trefoil and spandrels probably dating from between 1350 and 1450.

The chapel now houses the organ (1901 – by Alfred Oldknow) and the vestry. The latter is enclosed by an oak screen erected to the memory of Commander Edward Owen Obbard, D.S.C., G.M., R.N., Jurat, in 1951. It contains the oak altar table which was used in the days of the quarterly communions. Only two other such tables survive in the island. In the north wall, towards the east end, are two rectangular recesses, one of which was almost certainly an aumbry.

There are a number of mural memorials of which four are worth mentioning. The first, on the east wall of the south transept, is a black marble tablet streaked with white bearing a heart-rending inscription to the memory of Helier Dumaresq (died 1716) and Esther Dumaresq, his daughter (died 1717). The second, a fine brass with regimental crest on the top left-hand corner and decorated border, on the south wall of the chancel, is to William Arthur McCrae Bruce who won the Victoria Cross for gallantry at La Bassée, France, on 19 December 1914. The other two memorials are both marble tablets on the north wall of the chapel, within the vestry. One is to the memory of Philip Le Maistre (died 1848), Lord of Samarès Manor, his wife, and two of their daughters and has the Le Maistre coat of arms at its head; the other is to John Barbenson (died 1856), a native of Alderney and a churchwarden, of Constantia Lodge (now demolished), St Clement, and bears masonic emblems.

The windows vary greatly in size and shape and the majority of them contain stained glass. The two small windows on the north side of the nave contain glass presented by P. H. de Gruchy. The east side of the window to the west contains a figure of Sir Galahad and is dedicated to the memory of the Normans of "Hamptonne". Above the west door is a window to the memory of Mary Ann Le Brocq, her son Ernest, and her daughter, Mary Ann. The west and central windows in the south wall of the nave are dedicated to the memory of the Reverend Charles Walter Balleine, Rector of St Clement (1898–1932) and depicts respectively St Clement and St Nicholas. The east window is in memory of the Reverend Thomas Seale, Rector of St Clement (1729–46) and was presented in 1881. There is a small window in the east wall of the south transept filled with glass depicting the baptism of Jesus. The three windows in the chancel are all filled with stained glass. The east window, the finest in the church, was presented in 1881; the east window on the south side is to the memory of Charles Jean Benest, Jurat, who was Constable of St Clement for twenty-one years, and to Jane Ann Laverty, his wife, and was erected in 1926; the west window on the south side is to the memory of Philip Le Maistre, Lord of the Manor of St Ouen, and of Rachel d'Auvergne, his wife, and was erected in 1882.

The church has one bell inscribed around the shoulder "Saint Clement Island of Jersey 10th August 1828 John Touzel and Gideon Ahier Church Wardens" and around the lip "Made by Marquet Bellfounder of Villedieu Sold by Pierre Le Lièvre and Gabriel Guillaume living at Villedieu" (translations from French).

The parish registers are preserved from 1623.

The church stands in a well-cared-for churchyard in which are a number of trees including a splendid yew to the south of the church and a fine lime close to the north-west corner of the building.

The only memorial worth mentioning is to be found against the exterior of the south wall of the chancel beneath the southeast window. It takes the form of a chest tomb surmounted by a slab of Mont Mado granite two feet three inches square on which are carved four shields surrounded by the legend "LAN 1596 JEAN DM + ESTER DUM LAN 1606", recording John and Ester Dumaresq, his wife, Lady of the Manor of Samarès. The shields bear the trefoils of the Payns, the scallop shells of the Dumaresqs, the dolphins of the de Bagots and the dimidiated arms of the Payns and Lemprières (three eagles displayed).

The external features of the church worth noting are almost

exclusively confined to the chancel. They are: a gargoyle at the north-east corner of the gable, crockets along the gable end, a shield above the decorative motif at the top of the east window and two incised gravestones built into the lower part of the east wall. The presence of the Payn Arms inside the chancel and a somewhat elaborate memorial incorporating the Payn Arms against the exterior of the south wall and possibly the Payn Arms on the shield high up on the east gable might lead one to suppose that a member of the family was responsible for some work on the church, possibly the rebuilding of the east gable of the chancel with its fine window and the arcade between the chancel and the chapel to the north.

The main entrance to the churchyard is through a gateway with iron gates supported by granite pillars. To the left (looking from the road) is a stile comprising a short flight of granite steps on the outer and inner sides of the churchyard wall allowing pedestrian access when the gates are closed.

Let into the exterior face of the south-east corner of the churchyard wall is the announcement box with a grilled front where official notices are displayed.

Close by the church, to the south-west of the churchyard, stood the priory of St Clement which has long since disappeared. It is believed that it stood approximately on the site now occupied by the granite house called The Priory which has a square stone over the front door inscribed "C.T.E.M. 1814". The first set of initials is above the second and the second is above the date.

To the east of the church, on the far side of La Rue Laurens, is the Caldwell Hall, now the church hall and formerly the parish hall, built in 1878.

ST JOHN'S CHURCH (St John-in-the-Oaks) is bounded on the south by St John's main road, on the east by a pedestrian precinct and on the west by La Route du Nord.

The church, which is known to have existed as early as 1150, has a two-storeyed belfry surmounted by a spire from which the external cement rendering was removed 1972–73. The western face of the spire bears the arms (nine billets of wood) of Thomas Lemprière, Lord of the Manor of La

Hougue Boëte, bailiff in 1495. The spire is topped by a weathercock (1774) and the belfry has a striking clock (1968) on its southern face. The building is stone-vaulted and roofed with slate. The interior consists of a nave, south aisle, chancel, chancel aisle (1853) and vestry (1971 – by Taylor Leapingwell).

The names of all the known rectors starting with Richard Guesdel (between 1294 and probably 1297) are engraved on a slate slab (1974) by the west door.

A pillar was removed from the east end of the nave in 1849 in order to provide a better view of the pulpit – hence the double size arch.

The church is lit by fine brass chandeliers converted to electricity. The organ, installed in 1968, stands at the west end of the south aisle. At the east end of the same aisle there is a corbel on either side of the arch before the area under the belfry. The pulpit dates from 1791 but was cut down to its present size in 1921. Across the nave, just within the south aisle stands the fine brass lectern. The granite font stands on the south side of the church beneath the belfry. In the wall to the right of the entrance to the present vestry is a damaged holy water stoup. By the north end of the altar in the chancel is a blocked-up doorway.

On the south side of the church to the right of the door is a glass-fronted treasury (1975) in which is displayed the church's collection of silver. It is a memorial to the Reverend Leslie Sinclair-Lewis (1908–74), assistant Priest. The church's plate includes: six cups, a platter, a dish, a flagon bearing the London hallmark for 1850 and an aspersorium.

The church also possesses six pieces of pewter comprising: the earliest dated Jersey lidded pot flagon, bearing the maker's mark "P:D:R" (Pierre du Rousseau) and inscribed "DONNE A L'EGLISE DE SAIN IEAN 1718", and an unmarked and undated pot flagon inscribed "POVR LA PARROISSE DE ST. IAN", and four platters inscribed on the rim "POUR L'USAGE DE LA COMMUNION DE ST. JEAN", three are inscribed on the back "DNC / PLB } Survts" and the fourth "FEP / PEB } Survts".

The church has three collecting pots, one bearing the initials of Abraham de Carteret, the de Carteret Arms and the date 1677, stands on a granite pillar opposite the south door, the other two are probably eighteenth century.

The south-east window is filled with stained glass (1910) by Bosdet depicting St Michael and St Gabriel presented in memory of John Arthur Vaudin and Mary Ann Vaudin (née Pinel), his wife. In the south wall of the transept is a window presented by the Reverend E. St J. Nicolle who was rector for forty-six years. In the north wall of the nave, immediately to the west of the pulpit, is a window in memory of Ada Renouf Nicolle (née Le Boutillier), the Reverend Nicolle's widow (died 1956). There are two more stained-glass windows in the chancel: the east one presented by Miss Clara Valpy in memory of her family; the west one (1946) in memory of the Remeril family. Lastly, the rose window in the west gable is filled with stained glass (1972 – by John Stevens) presented by the Fallas of Les Issues.

Memorials to be noted are those to: Josué Le Couteur (died 1675); Abraham de Carteret (died 1681), Lord of the Manor of La Hougue Boëte – a fine granite stone with arms at head; Clement Lemprière (died 1715); General Helier Touzel (died 1865) – associated with the building of Victoria College, the abolition of Sunday elections and originator of St John's Central School.

The church has one bell cast in Jersey by Jacques Pitel in 1754, which was re-hung in 1967, and a ring of bells made by the Whitechapel Foundry and installed in 1979.

The parish registers date from 1594.

The glass doors giving access to the church from the south porch are engraved with Maltese crosses surrounded by acorns and oak leaves.

Over the outside of the blocked-up doorway to the north of the altar are carved the date "1622" and the initials "JLB" and from the gables gargoyles protrude their ugly faces.

The west wall of the churchyard is unusual in that it is composed of a number of small gravestones. Other memorials worth noting are the small water-worn boulders used as gravestones and the chest tomb to Jean Le Febvre (died 1651), Lord of La Hougue Boëte.

The fine granite-built parish hall (1912) stands across the road from the church on the corner of La Rue de la Mare Bellam and La Rue des Buttes.

ST LAWRENCE'S CHURCH is situated on St Lawrence's main road, its churchyard being bounded on the east by that thoroughfare and on its other three sides by other public roads. Geoffrey (before 1198) is the first recorded rector.

The church, which is known to have existed before 1198, is stone-vaulted and roofed with tiles. It has a Norman saddleback tower with a cross at the apex of each gable and Norman windows on each side at top floor level. The tower narrows noticeably at a point in line with the apex of the roof of the nave, which indicates that the section above that point is not the original. It would also appear that the tower was raised at the restoration of the church 1890–92. Access to the tower is gained by a stair-turret built at the same time as the Hamptonne Chapel.

The interior of the church consists of the nave, nave aisle (1546), crossing, north and south transepts and the Hamptonne Chapel. The nave is separated from the nave aisle by an arcade consisting of circular pillars with octagonal capitals. The north transept was rebuilt at the time of the construction of the Hamptonne Chapel.

The granite font stands at the west end of the nave to the right of the door. The vestry is on the north side of the nave aisle. There is a recess in the east wall of the south transept: against the west wall is the ancient communion table.

The Hamptonne Chapel (now the Lady Chapel), considered the finest example of ecclesiastical architecture in the island, was built in 1524 by Louis Hamptonne, Rector (1502–58), and the Hamptonne Arms, three stars, appear on a boss on the roof of the chapel and again outside with the date 1524 on the north-east buttress.

The chapel, in the Flamboyant Gothic style, has a groined roof with quadrilateral vaulting. As has been stated, one boss is carved with the Hamptonne Arms; another is carved with the Tudor Rose. In each of three corners of the chapel is a carved head, a man (north-west corner), a woman (north-east corner) and a girl (south-east corner), each with a head covering; the man has a beard. There would seem to be no doubt that three actual people are depicted. If this is the case, who are they? One possibility, particularly bearing in mind the date of the building of the chapel and the boss bearing the Tudor Rose, is that the three carvings are intended to represent King Henry VIII, Queen Catherine of Aragon and Princess Mary, later Queen Mary I. There is another head, this time a comic one, carved on a corbel in the south-west corner of the north transept.

The chapel is divided from the chancel by pointed arches springing from octagonal pillars without capitals. A large arch of the same type divides the chapel from the east side of the north transept, which was enlarged and roofed in the same style as the chapel. The southern pillar of this arch has a small rectangular opening pierced through it.

There is a piscina in the south wall of the chapel, near the south-east corner, to the right of where the altar once stood, beneath the east window.

The outstanding possession of the church is a granite stone, semicircular in section, found with its broken end uppermost, two or three feet below the nave in 1891. The stone formed the upper part of an engaged or applied column of the Doric order in a third- or fourth-century Roman villa. About 600 it had its flat head used for an epitaph, and finally in the eighth or ninth century it had its back carved with a decorative design. Despite examination by several experts no definitive interpretation of the epitaph has yet been made. It is safe to say that the stone originated outside Jersey and the villa of which it formed part did not stand in the island. It is not known whether the epitaph and the decorative design were carved on the stone in Jersey or elsewhere. It could well have been that it was brought to the island as it is to-day, but for what reason it is impossible to say. However, its presence beneath the church, as well as the very ancient gravestones built into the exterior walls of the building, would indicate that a Christian church stood on the site of St Lawrence's Church from as early as the seventh century.

The church possesses a number of stained-glass windows.

The east window depicting "The Last Supper" is by Bosdet, who in his latter years lived in the parish in the beautiful thatched house Le Patrimoine, destroyed by fire in 1963. The east window of the Hamptonne Chapel depicting "Christ in a Fishing Boat on the Lake of Galilee" is by Walter Skeet and was given in memory of Commander Redvers Prior, D.S.O., D.S.C., R.N. The window at the east end on the south side of the chancel was presented by the officers of the St Lawrence Battalion of the Royal Jersey Militia on its disbandment in 1877. The two windows to the right contain stained glass depicting St Lawrence washing the feet of Christians, raising a widow to life and baptizing the jailer; also the saint's martyrdom. The window in the north transept was presented anonymously in 1969. In the west light is depicted St Cecilia, the patron saint of music, with an angel below; in the east is the Virgin Mary together with a small choirboy, with an angel below. In the top are depicted the arms of the Royal College of Music. The window in the south transept also dates from 1969 and depicts St Anthony and St Swithun with coats of arms above. The two-light window at the west end of the north aisle is in memory of Elizabeth Le Couteur (née Valpy) (died 1918) and has as its subjects "The Light of the World" and "The Good Shepherd". The few surviving fragments of the church's medieval stained glass are in the small window above the west door.

In the church are preserved two sets of colours of the St Lawrence Battalion of the Fourth Regiment of the Royal Jersey Militia, the first probably dating from the second decade of the nineteenth century and the second from 1841.

The church plate includes: four cups, one with the London hallmark for 1598, a damaged dish, a baptismal dish, probably by Jean Gruchy, two platters, two further platters and a flagon bearing the London hallmark for 1843. The church owns a collection of pewter, all made by John de Ste Croix, a Jersey pewterer. The collection comprises three Jersey flagons, two pots and a pint, bearing on their handles the inscription "ST LORAIN", a plate, and two alms dishes both inscribed on the back "ST. LR". It also owns two old copper collecting pots and two oak alms dishes presented in 1969.

The church has the oldest bell in Jersey. It is inscribed "This bell is for the Parish of St. Lawrence in Jersey A.D. 1592 IW" (translation from the French). Presumably the initials "IW" are those of John Wallis of Salisbury.

The church registers are preserved from 1654.

Exterior features of the Hamptonne Chapel worth noting are the crockets along the gables, the cross at the apex of each gable, the dripstones above the windows, the decorative buttresses and gargoyles; also the stair-turret giving access to the tower.

A number of ancient gravestones have been built into the exterior walls of the church. Two are in the buttress at the east end, between the chancel and the Hamptonne Chapel. On the upper one is depicted a cross and on the lower an unidentifiable design. Another two have been built into the buttress against the east wall close to the south-east corner. On the upper one is depicted an unidentifiable design and on the lower a cross. Another has been built into the front of the east buttress on the south side of the chancel and possibly another into the west face. A face possibly but not necessarily from a tombstone has been built into the front of the centre buttress. There is also an old gravestone, built into the west side of the same buttress. Finally, a gravestone on which is depicted a cross design is built into the front of the west buttress.

Those gravestones with a circle at the intersection of the cross are considered to be Celtic of the ninth century; that bearing a design composed of intersecting triangles and other symbols is considered to date from the ninth or tenth century; those with a cross standing on a stepped base, date from the twelfth century.

In the exterior of the south wall of the chancel is a granite memorial to Lawrence Hamptonne (1660–64), Viscount (Sheriff) and his son Edward Hamptonne (1628–60), who was also Viscount, with the family arms at the head and the motto 'All is dust' in Greek. The inscription is in Latin. There are a number of old gravestones outside the south wall of the nave, the most notable being an elaborate one in granite to Nicolas de Tréguz (died 1586).

There are two doorways in the west front of the church. It is said that the north one was built as wide as it is to allow the parish cannons to be brought in and out in the days when they were housed in the church. Between the two doorways is a flattened buttress with an unusual dragon drain head above it. Above the south door is a sundial, and to the right of the same door is a poor-box.

At the south-east corner of the churchyard is a lychgate (1910) erected in memory of Jennet Susannah Collas (née Balleine) by her husband Elias Collas.

Across the road to the north of the church stands the parish hall.

ST MARTIN'S CHURCH (St Martin-the-Old) is situated at the corner of La Rue de Croix au Maitre and La Grande Route de Rozel, St Martin. Robert de la Hougue (?–1196) is the first recorded rector.

The church, which is known to have existed in 1042, is stone-vaulted, roofed with red tiles, and has a remarkable number of buttresses supporting its walls. It has a central tower with an octagonal spire, surmounted by a weathercock, and a clock (1903) commemorating the coronation of King Edward VII let into its southern face. The west door has a porch. The interior of the church consists of a nave, south aisle, the Mabon Chapel (west end) on the north side of the crossing, where a north transept would ordinarily be found, chancel and a chapel to the south of the chancel, divided from the south aisle by a screen (1969) in memory of the Reverend Edward Cecil Lemprière, a former rector.

The font is located in the nave close to the west door. A granite corbel protrudes from the wall at the back of the pulpit. At the east end of the south aisle stands a splendid brass lectern with steps to match (1903) presented by W. A. Sohier. An ancient wooden statue of St Martin dividing his cloak with a beggar, presented by Lady Trent, stands against the north wall of the chancel. On the north side of the sanctuary stands the bishop's chair and prie-dieu. The building contains the remains of at least three piscinae.

All the windows in the church contain stained glass,

although four, three on the south side of the chapel and one
on the south side of the south aisle, only contain patterned
glass. Three windows are by Bosdet including "The Annunciation" adjacent to the pulpit. The fine west window (*"Ecce
Homo"*) of the south aisle is by Curteis, and was presented by
Miss A. M. Amy in 1903. The east window of the chancel
("The Ascension") was presented by the Reverend William
Lemprière, Lord of Rozel Manor. The east window of the
chapel depicts "The Adoration". The window on the south
side of the south aisle depicting "St Paul preaching at Athens"
was presented by twenty-three churchwardens who held
office from 1750–1890!

The regimental colours of the Second or East Regiment of
the Royal Jersey Militia, presented about 1879 and laid up in
1925, are preserved in two glass-fronted frames attached to
the west wall of the nave.

The church owns the following plate; four cups, one by the
Jersey maker with the mark "IG", a further cup and a salver
bearing the Exeter or Edinburgh hallmark for 1861, and a
paten with a foot and a flagon, both dated 1877; also three collecting pots.

The church used also to own a pewter dish by John de Ste
Croix bearing an inscription stating that it was given in 1738
(probably the year of manufacture) to replace a gift by Francis
Le Couteur, Rector, made in 1673. It is now in the Jersey
Museum.

The church has one bell bearing an inscription in French
stating that its name is Martin and that it was founded in
London in 1768 by Lester & Pack.

The church registers are preserved from early in the 1590s.

A number of ancient gravestones have been built into the
exterior of the building. There is a curious carved face above
the east window of the Mabon Chapel; there is another on the
south wall of the main church. On the south side there is a
sundial (1736) presented by George Bandinel, the Viscount
(Sheriff). On the buttress to the left of the sundial there is an
elaborate   heraldic   monument,   unfortunately   much
weathered. It consists of a shield with two human supporters,
within an arch with two crudely carved human heads. The

finial of the arch appears to be a chalice supported by a winged angel and there is an animal's head on each shoulder of the arch. There is a gargoyle at the east end and another at the west end. The south-west corner of the churchyard is occupied by the granite war memorial (1924 – by Charles de Gruchy).

ST MARY'S CHURCH (St Mary of the Burnt Monastery) is situated at the corner of La Grande Route de Ste Marie and La Rue de la Vallée. The reference to a burnt monastery implies that the church stands on or near the site of a religious house that was burnt, probably during a raid on the island. Robert Florie (1185–1208) is the first recorded rector although on the list of incumbents appearing on the west wall of the nave aisle the earliest is given as Guillaume de Marchia (1298).

The church, which is known to have existed in 1042, is stone-vaulted and roofed with slate. It has a central tower with a hexagonal spire surmounted by a weathercock. At each corner of the tower is a square pinnacle open on rounded arches. The north-east pinnacle bears the date 1834. In the tower is a clock with two faces, one on the north front and one on the east. The church consists of a nave, nave aisle, chancel and a Lady Chapel (the oldest part of the building) on the north side of the chancel. In the east wall of the chancel, behind the altar, are two corbels, one to the left and one to the right; in the east wall of the Lady Chapel are the remains of two Norman windows. There is a fine piscina to the right of the altar, which it is believed dates from the middle of the fourteenth century and has clusters of rope moulding at its shoulders. There is also an aumbry or an Easter sepulchre to the left of the altar and a holy water stoup let into the south wall about a third of the way from the east end of the church. Other things worth noting are the ancient communion table and the modern granite font.

The church has a number of stained-glass windows including two in memory of members of the Collas family by Bosdet in the south wall. There are three recently installed windows on the north side: in the Lady Chapel "The Annunciation" in memory of Norman Harrison (1873–1949) and Marguerite Ethel Harrison (née Dorey) (1875–1953), his wife; in the nave aisle "I am the Light of the World" in memory of Lieutenant Edward Renouf who died of wounds (1916) and "Give Ye Them to Eat" in memory of Anna, John and Olive Renouf.

The church has the following memorials: Daniel Gruchy, Rector (died 1677) – slate with stone surround with angel's head; a fine memorial, with arms at its head, on the south wall to Thomas Le Breton, Rector and Dean (died 1728); Le Couteur Balleine, Rector (died 1879).

In the church are preserved in glass-fronted frames the regimental colours of the First or West Regiment of the Royal Jersey Militia, presented in 1879 and laid up in 1925.

The church plate includes: two cups, two mazer-type bowls, paten on foot with London hallmark for 1851 and a flagon with London hallmark for 1855. The church also owns two collecting pots, one dated 1812.

The church bell dates from 1910 and was cast at Villedieu. It shares the belfry with four small bells cast by John Warner & Sons, London, in 1888 which belong to the striking clock given by Miss A. M. Vibert the same year. The bell, like those at St Ouen and St Peter, are rung, subject to certain breaks, from midday on Christmas Eve until midnight on Christmas Day.

The church registers are preserved from 1647.

Let into the outside of the west wall of the church is an ancient gravestone incised with the likeness of a priest, a chalice and a fish. There is a stone bearing the date 1342 in Roman numerals on the apex of the gable of the chancel. On the south wall is a sundial (1763) bearing the inscription "*Ut umbra sic vita 1763*", and projecting from the east wall is a gargoyle.

ST OUEN'S CHURCH is situated at Ville de l'Eglise, St Ouen. The first recorded rector is Etienne (Stephanus) (1156).

The church, which is known to have existed not later than 1066, is stone-vaulted and roofed with slates. It has a central tower with long narrow slits for light at its base. The tower has a spire surmounted by a weathercock. The interior of the building consists of a nave with two aisles and a chancel with a chapel on either side. The north and south transepts have been absorbed into the chancel and the chapels.

An unusual feature of the nave is the stone staircase giving access to the belfry. The pulpit is of Caen stone with panels enclosed by marble pillars. The lectern is of oak and was made by James Alexandre; the font is of granite and was the gift of Philip Le Feuvre. The organ was installed in 1963.

The east window contains medallions depicting "St John the Baptist", "The Crucifixion" and "Christ Blessing the Children". Some of the stained glass in the church is of poor quality and the colour has disappeared in places. The west window also contains medallions depicting "Adam and Eve", "The Deluge" and "The Sacrifice of Abel".

Among a number of other memorials is a brass to Sir Philip de Carteret (1583–1643) and another, also in brass (1872), to a branch of the de Carteret family. On the east wall of the north chapel is the marble top of a chest tomb in which was buried Elizabeth Wilson, the seven-year-old daughter of Robert Wilson, Lieutenant-Governor of Jersey, who died in 1719.

In the church is preserved the regimental colour of the First or North-West Regiment of the Royal Jersey Militia, presented in 1851 and laid up in 1882.

The church plate includes: a cup (formerly gilt) bearing a Nuremberg mark; two cups bearing the London hallmark for 1638, of particular interest because they were presented by Captain (later Sir) George Carteret, (Bt); two cups bearing respectively the London hallmarks for 1624 and 1627; cup bearing the London hallmark for 1640; cup converted into a flagon and bearing the London hallmark for 1635; flagon bearing the London hallmark (year indistinct); two platters bearing respectively the London hallmarks for 1638 and 1676; baptismal dish bearing the London hallmark for 1806; a paten on foot bearing the mark of a Jersey silversmith "PB" under a crown; paten bearing the London hallmark for 1910.

The church has one bell re-cast by John Taylor & Sons at Loughborough in 1971. Its predecessor was cast by Gabriel

Guillaume in 1844 and replaced one cast in Bristol in 1812 which in turn replaced a bell cast by one La Source in 1754. The bell, like those at St Mary and St Peter, are rung, subject to certain breaks, from midday on Christmas Eve until midnight on Christmas Day.

The church registers are preserved from 1634.

The exterior of the church has certain features worth noting. In the porch on either side of the door are carved two primitive faces: the one on the right has a beard. Over the windows are ornamental dripstones featuring various motifs: animals, fleurs-de-lis, portcullises. At least three old gravestones have been built into the fabric, one depicting a patriarchal cross into the south-east buttress, another depicting a chalice and book under the south-east window and yet another bearing a cross.

The west front has angle buttresses and the apex of the centre gable terminates not in a cross but a chimney pot!

At the eastern end of the south chapel is a granite stone to the memory of Peter de la Place, Rector, who died in 1681. At the top of the stone is carved a primitive face, presumably intended to depict the deceased.

There are two gargoyles at the west end of the church.

ST PETER'S CHURCH (St Peter in *'le Désert'*) is situated at Rue de l'Eglise, St Peter. The first recorded rector is Nicolas Galicien (before 1292).

The church, which is known to have existed at least as early as 1066, is stone-vaulted and roofed with tiles. It has a central tower with a quadrilateral spire, the highest in the island, rising to a height of over 120 feet. Owing to the close proximity of the church to the airport there are red lights at the top of the spire, lit at night and at other times as a warning to aircraft. There are windows in the tower at first-floor level and long narrow slits in the second storey. The spire was struck by lightning in 1612, 1843 and 1848. In the eastern face of the tower is a clock, unusual in the fact that it strikes the hour twice, a three-minute interval between each strike.

The interior of the church consists of a nave, with two aisles, north transept (now the Lady Chapel), crossing, south

transept occupied by the organ and library, north-east chapel
(now divided into a sacristy and flower room) and the choir
vestry (1967) at the west end of the south aisle. The north
aisle was added to the nave in 1886 and replaced an aisle
which did not extend the whole length of the nave. At the
time the church served as a garrison church for St Peter's Barracks, now demolished.

The two narrow lancet windows in the west wall of the nave
are original. The circular window was inserted in the 1850s.
Only a few of the windows contain stained glass.

The font dates from 1835, and in the north wall of the Lady
Chapel adjacent to the altar is a *bénitier* removed from a
house demolished for airport development. There is a piscina
in the south wall of the south aisle at its eastern end. Lighting
is provided by attractive lantern lights.

The reredos behind the altar in the chancel was presented
by the Reverend P. A. Lefèvre about 1887. It is made of
terracotta and is the work of George Tinworth (1843–1913), a
renowned artist of the Royal Doulton Potteries, in whose
Lambeth studios it was created. The reredos depicts "The
Last Supper" and bears the following biblical quotation: "I
say unto you that one of you shall betray me. And they were
exceeding sorrowful and began everyone of them to say unto
Him, Lord, is it I? Peter said unto Him, though I should die
with Thee, yet will I not deny Thee. Likewise also said they
all."

On the north wall of the chancel is another terracotta panel
by Tinworth, almost as large as the reredos illustrating the
text: "Jesus said to Simon Peter, Simon son of Jonas, lovest
thou me? And he said unto Him, Lord thou knowest all
things. Thou knowest that I love Thee."

Five icons are incorporated in the reredos at the back of the
altar in the Lady Chapel. Above the reredos is a statue of the
Virgin Mary and the baby Jesus made at L'Etacq Woodcrafts,
St Ouen.

Let into the floor at what was the north-east chapel is an
ancient tombstone, carved with a cross with a flamboyant
head. On the north wall to the left of the door is a cartouche
memorial to the memory of Elias de Carteret (died 1640) and

Elizabeth de Carteret (née Dumaresq), his wife (died 1639). The centre is of black marble, the surround is of pink veined marble and a small insert at the base is of grey marble. At the head of the memorial are carved the de Carteret Arms. The church also contains a number of Dumaresq memorials, also a large seventeenth-century memorial to Clement Le Montais who is stated on the inscription as being a rich merchant.

The church plate includes: four cups (two pairs), two flagons bearing the London hallmark for 1833, oval platter bearing the London hallmark for 1646, dish, baptismal dish by Pierre Amiraux, the Jersey silversmith, dish with London maker's mark – the date is indistinct, two patens bearing the London hallmark for 1883.

The church has two bells, the successors of 'Elisabeth' and 'Marie' which dated from 1649 and 1754 respectively. The former was re-cast in 1872 and the latter in 1873, both at Ville-dieu. The older is inscribed "*Mon Nom est Elisabeth la Belle*" and the younger "*Mon Nom est Marie la Cousine d'Elisabeth la Belle*". The bells, like that at St Mary's and St Ouen's are rung, subject to certain breaks, from midday on Christmas Eve until midnight on Christmas Day.

The church registers are preserved from 1626.

There is a sundial on the exterior of the south transept.

Two ancient gravestones have been built into the archway of the entrance at the centre of the west front. The one on the left is incised with a circle and a line; the one on the right has a stepped calvary. Another ancient gravestone has been built into the buttress between the west doors. On it are incised an ornamental cross, a hammer, a pair of pincers and what looks like two horseshoes (see de la Croix's *Antiquités* Vol. I, p. 286). It has been suggested that the gravestone commemorates a farrier, but this is probably not the case. In fact the hammer and pincers are numbered among the instruments of Christ's passion and the gravestone may be that of anyone. The end of each shaft of the cross is itself a cross and there is a circle at the intersection of the arms and the upright of the cross.

The parish hall stands alongside the east side of the churchyard.

ST SAVIOUR'S CHURCH (St Saviour of the Thorn) is situated on St Saviour's Hill a short distance past Government House. The name 'St Saviour of the Thorn' is first mentioned in the *Mémoires de la famille La Cloche* written in the seventeenth century. Johan Hue (1461–1507) is the first recorded rector.

The church, which is known to have existed at least as early as 1087, is stone-vaulted and roofed with tiles. It has a central tower with a battlemented parapet and a stair turret. It has three gargoyles of Chausey granite. There was a fourth at the south-east corner which has been broken off. The tower has windows in its top storey and a clock with two faces, one on the north side and the other on the south. The clock was presented in 1876 in memory of General Helier Touzel. The granite surrounds of the two faces were designed by J. Hayward.

The church consists of a nave, north aisle, crossing, north and south transept, chancel and Lady Chapel. The south transept houses the vestry.

It is said that the church grew from four separate chapels, but this seems unlikely. The point is discussed by Mr F. de L. Bois in his book on the church.

Practically the whole of the inside walls have been stripped of their plaster resulting in the building being dark inside even on the brightest day.

Built into the west wall of the nave, to the right of the door, is the treasury (1978) containing the church's collection of plate which includes: a platter bearing the London hallmark for 1699; two alms dishes with the London hallmark (possibly for 1684); a baptismal dish bearing the London hallmark for 1718; two chalices bearing the London hallmark for 1739; a paten on foot bearing the London hallmark for 1740 presented by Philip Falle, the Jersey historian who was Rector 1690–1706; two chalices and a flagon bearing the London hallmark for 1807, flagon bearing the London hallmark for 1808; a private communion set and wine strainer dated 1826; a private communion set dated 1846; communion cup bearing the Sheffield Silver Jubilee (1935) hallmark; five alms dishes bearing the Chester Silver Jubilee (1935) hallmark; a com-

munion cup and paten bearing the London hallmark for 1951;
a cross set with amethysts and two candlesticks 1957; a ciborium and cover and a wafer box dated 1969; private communion set presented 1973.

The church also has two carved oak alms dishes with fretted
covers fixed with bayonet fittings. One is inscribed *"Dieu
aime celui qui donne gaiement"*; the other "God loveth a
cheerful giver".

On the south side of the western end of the nave aisle stands
the nineteenth-century font of Mont Mado granite.

There is a carved figure of a man above the capital on the
north side of the westernmost arch of the nave arcade and
there are the remains of another carved figure above the south
side of the same capital. There is also a carved face on a cove-
moulded corbel let into the south wall of the nave.

The crossing is very like that at St Helier's Church. The
pulpit is of oak on a granite base. There are two lecterns, one
takes the form of a pelican feeding her young and the other of
an angel standing on a Gothic-style base. In front of the
chancel and the Lady Chapel are oak screens and there is
another dividing the chancel from the Lady Chapel.

There are the remains of what was probably a sedilia in the
south wall of the chancel. In passing it should be mentioned
that a sedilia was a range of seats, usually of stone and three in
number, on the south side of the chancel for the use of the
celebrant and his assistants, the deacon and sub-deacon,
during the Creed and Gloria when the service was sung. The
seats are either on the level or graded towards the east.

All the windows are filled with stained glass. The oldest
(1885) is the east window on the north wall of the Lady
Chapel which was given by Miss Rosalie Anne Le Geyt. The
two three-light windows, one on the north side of the nave
and the other on the south, were given by Jurat J. G. Falle.
The four-light east window of the Lady Chapel depicts
"Christ and the Fishermen in the Sea of Galilee". The east
window of the chancel depicts "Christ carrying the Cross",
"Christ on the Cross" and "Christ enthroned in Heaven".
Bosdet designed the east and west windows in the south wall
of the chancel as well as the two windows in the west gables;

he also painted the panel in the reredos.

The church is rich in mural tablets and space forbids mention of more than a few. There is one with a Latin inscription to John Poingdestre (died 1691), a very distinguished Jerseyman who became Lieutenant-Bailiff. There are two fine memorials to members of the La Cloche family. That on the south wall of the chancel commemorates George La Cloche (died 1681) and has his arms at its head: that on the north wall of the Lady Chapel commemorates Amice La Cloche (died 1725) and Anne La Cloche (née Seale), his wife (died 1759). A tablet on the north wall of the Lady Chapel is to the memory of General Sir Lothian Nicholson, K.C.B., R.E., Lieutenant-Governor of Jersey 1878–83. Another tablet on the north wall of the same chapel is to the memory of Lillie Langtry (1853–1929) and records that she was baptized, twice married and buried in the parish and that it was erected by her only child Jeanne.

In the church are preserved the regimental colours of the Third or East Regiment of the Royal Jersey Militia, presented in 1871 and laid up a few years later. They hang within the west arch of the crossing.

The church possesses a peal of four bells. The oldest bears a Latin inscription stating that it was bought through the private contributions of individuals, weighs 1,150 pounds, was hung in 1656 and was made by Martin Huard. The other three given in memory of Carlyle Le Gallais were made at the Whitechapel Bell Foundry in 1968.

The church registers commence as follows: baptisms 1540, burials 1541 and marriages 1542.

There is a niche at the south-west corner of the church with a scallop shell at its head and the initials "GL", believed to be those of George Lemprière, Constable of St Saviour in 1464, who made the pilgrimage to the shrine of St James of Compostella. There is a corresponding niche at the north-west corner on which are carved the Lemprière Arms, three eagles displayed.

Parts of old gravestones have been built into the exterior fabric of the church, notably three examples on the outside of the Lady Chapel, one clearly depicts the stepped base of a cross; another depicts the head of a cross; yet another would appear to depict the head of a cross.

Above the larger window in the south wall of the south transept is a sundial, and to the right of the door in the same wall is an old poor-box. There is a gargoyle between the gable ends of the chancel and the Lady Chapel and another on the west front.

The churchyard is large and contains a great many gravestones and memorials. One states that the deceased died "Most Mysteriously", another that the deceased is "Wanted". Beneath the three-light window of the nave, is another of Mont Mado granite commemorating John Pallot (1577–1661), Master of St Mannelier School, and Jeanne Fautrat (15?0–1670), his wife. A broken pillar in Caen stone erected in 1849 commemorates David Ross Dixon (died 1848), an engineer employed by Messrs Jackson Bros., contractors, in connection with the harbour works at St Catherine's, who was killed in an accident. A memorial in the form of a chest tomb commemorates Thomas Le Hardy, miniaturist (1771–1813) and his parents. A large marble cannon commemorates Major-General John Lawrence Bolton (died 1896) of the Royal Artillery who served in the Crimea and the Indian Mutiny. A granite headstone commemorates Henry Kemble (1848–1907), the actor. The most famous person commemorated in the churchyard is undoubtedly Lillie Langtry (1853–1929), who is buried in the family grave. There on a granite plinth is a bust of Lillie carved in white marble, bearing her name and the dates of her birth and death. In the same grave are buried her father, William Corbet Le Breton (died 1888), Rector of St Saviour and Dean of Jersey, and Emilie Davis Le Breton (née Martin), her mother, who are commemorated by a marble cross on a rough-hewn base standing on a two-tier smooth granite plinth with inscriptions.

The lychgate was erected to the memory of George Orange Balleine, Dean of Jersey (1888–1906).

Let into the outer side of the churchyard wall on either side of the lychgate are the parish notice boxes.

Princess Margaret visited the church in October 1977.

The present rectory, built of Mont Mado granite, replaced

the old rectory, where Lillie Langtry was born on 13 October 1853. The latter was sold in 1961 and is now a private residence.

TRINITY CHURCH is situated at the corner of La Rue-ès-Picots and La Rue du Presbytère, Trinity.

The church, which is known to have existed in 1090, is stone-vaulted and roofed with slate. It has a central tower and spire with weathercock, rendered in cement with slits in the belfry. In the southern face of the tower is a clock "Set going July 4th 1883 by Miss Martha Messervy". The interior consists of a nave, chancel, Lady Chapel, north transept and south porch.

The interior is very plain. The centre pillar of the arcade dividing the chancel from the chapel to the north was removed in 1830 to improve the view of the pulpit. The font dates from 1851.

The altar stone came from Mont Orgueil Castle where a number of such stones, removed from churches and chapels at the Reformation, were built into the fabric. It stands on a bow-shaped granite pedestal, the front of which is supported by two octagonal granite pillars. A relic of King Charles I (a piece of braid from one of the shoes he wore at his execution) and other items are sealed in the pedestal. On the altar stand a cross and candlesticks of beaten copper in memory of the Starck family of Trinity.

There is a list of the rectors on a board on the west wall of the south porch. Nicolas de Cumbervill (1298–?) is the first recorded rector.

There is a stained-glass window in the south wall of the chancel to the memory of Jurat A. Messervy.

The finest memorial in the church, and finest seventeenth-century memorial in the island, is that to Sir Edward de Carteret, Gentleman Usher of the Black Rod (died 1683), against the north wall of the Lady Chapel, where it was moved in 1854. At the head of the memorial are de Carteret's armorial bearings. The shield displays on the dexter side the arms of de Carteret and on the sinister the arms of Johnson, Lady Elizabeth de Carteret being the daughter of Robert Johnson,

Alderman of London. There are three memorial slabs let into the floor of the chancel as follows: Philippe Le Boutillier (died 1665), Hugh Lemprière, Lord of the Manor of Diélament (died 1685) and Denis Guerdain (died 1742) and Sara Guerdain (née Richardson), his wife (died 1746).

The church plate includes: the bowl and the base of a pre-Reformation chalice, a reproduction of the complete chalice bearing the London hallmark for 1912, six cups, two platters, an alms dish bearing the London hallmark for 1834 and a paten bearing the London hallmark for 1912.

The church also owns two processional candlesticks and a copper collecting-pot.

The church has one bell bearing an inscription stating that it was founded in 1690 in the reign of William and Mary, the names of the rector, constable and the two centeniers and four shields bearing the arms of Dumaresq, de Carteret, Lempière and Guerdain. The bell was cast by Paul Bourdon.

The church registers are preserved from 1612.

On a stone let into the exterior of the church are carved the arms of John Dumaresq, dated 1601, and standing close to the church wall is a large memorial stone with the arms of de Carteret and the Trinity branch of the Lemprière family at its head, to the memory of Charles de Carteret (died 1685) and Mary de Carteret, his first wife (died 1681).

The war memorial takes the form of a lychgate (1951 – by A. Le Sueur) giving access to the churchyard from La Rue du Presbytère.

2

Guernsey's Ancient Parish Churches

ST PETER PORT CHURCH, often referred to as the 'Town Church' as it is situated at the foot of the High Street in the town of St Peter Port, is devoid of a churchyard and surrounded on all sides by public thoroughfares. Pierre Le Valleys (1282) is the first recorded rector.

The church, which is the finest ancient parish church in the Channel Islands, is known to have existed in about 1048. It is stone-vaulted and has a central tower, with a battlemented parapet and a gargoyle at each corner, and a spire surmounted by a weathercock. The tower contains a clock (1781) with four faces and the lead-covered spire bears an inscription, the cross keys of St Peter and the date 1721. The clock bell weighing 14 hundredweights and probably dating from 1736 hangs under a canopy on the north side of the spire. Access to the tower is obtained by way of a stair turret located at the point where the west wall of the south transept meets the south wall of the nave and with its door opening into the nave. The interior of the church consists of a nave with a north and south aisle, crossing, north and south transept (the latter bearing the date 1466), and a chancel with a chapel on its north side and another on its south side. The roof of the nave and chancel is groined. The pointed arches of the nave are plain and heavy compared with those of the chancel and south transept and spring from nearer the ground.

The bailiff's pew, the front pew on the south side of the nave, is carved with the arms of Guernsey and those of Sir Edgar MacCulloch, Bailiff 1884–95, as well as the inscription "By manhood and with spirit" (translation from Latin). The font of Purbeck marble stands at the west end of the north aisle of the nave and was given in memory of Havilland Carey.

The crossing with its massive pillars is stone-vaulted. On the north side of the north door is a list of the rectors of St Peter Port from early times to the present day. The pulpit of carved alabaster and Caen stone was given in memory of Jurat Henri Tupper in 1886. The brass eagle lectern was given in memory of Peter Le Lièvre.

The chancel is divided from the nave by a wrought-iron screen with gates. On the riser of the sanctuary step is inscribed "Come unto Me all ye that labour and are heavy laden and I will give you rest" and on the sanctuary floor is inscribed "Each time you drink from this cup you will proclaim the death of the Lord until He comes again". Both inscriptions are in French. There are twelve carved panels depicting scenes in the life of St Peter on the choir stalls. On the north side of the sanctuary is the bishop's throne given in memory of John George Renier and Eliza Renier (née Petherick), his wife. There are also the dean's stall and the rector's stall. The altar (by J. Pippet) was given in memory of Robert Seeds. The ornate reredos and the walnut screens dividing the chancel from the Brock Memorial Chapel and the chapel on the south side were given in memory of the Reverend William Thomas Collings. The reredos was redecorated in 1939 and the three centre panels were filled with paintings in memory of Cecil Augustus Carey. The centre painting is of the Holy Family, the other two are of the Adoration of the Kings and of the Adoration of the Shepherds. The two panels on either side of the three centre panels have painted at their base a shortened form of the Commandments in French. An icon brought from Sebastopol in 1855 hangs on the centre pillar on the north side.

On the north side of the chancel is the Brock Memorial Chapel or Lady Chapel. At its entrance is a screen to the memory of Major-General Sir Isaac Brock who saved Canada on 13 October 1812. There is also a screen dividing the chapel from the chancel. The altar was given in memory of Gerald Hatton Carey; the cross and candlesticks were given in memory of Doris Blad; the matching pair of vases were given by the Mothers' Union in 1957.

On the south side of the chancel is another chapel in which

the organ is located. The present instrument was restored by Maley Young & Oldham late last century, rebuilt by Hele & Son in 1929, and completely overhauled and renovated by Walker & Sons in 1960.

The church has the following piscinae: two behind the reredos, one in the Brock Chapel with a beautiful Caen stone credence close by, one behind the organ and the last close to the door leading to the vestries.

Most of the stained-glass windows were shattered during World War II, but despite this the church contains a number of them. Above the High Altar is the magnificent Liberation Window (1949 – by Harry Gyles) with the theme *Te Deum Laudamus*, incorporating the arms of the bailiwick and those of the diocese of Winchester. Above the altar in the Brock Chapel is a window (1948) to the memory of William Prelaz Grousaz, O.B.E., Jurat and organist of St Peter Port Church for 47 years. It depicts "The Presentation of Christ in the Temple" (by Donald Taunton). The two windows on the north side of the chapel depict respectively "The Nativity" and "The Annunciation" (1953 – by Taunton). The top part of the window in the north transept is original: the lower part which is post-war, depicts St Peter walking on the sea (1953 – by Taunton). There are two lancet windows in the north wall of the baptistry, one depicting St John the Baptist baptizing Christ, in memory of Sophie Rachel de Putron (née Rousell) wife of Daniel de Putron, and the other depicting Christ's conversation with Nicodemus, in memory of the Reverend Pierre Carey, Rector of St Saviour (1843–74), and Marianne Carey (née Maingay), his wife.

The church is the 'Westminster Abbey' of Guernsey and its walls are lined with numerous memorials. Among those commemorated are: Robert Bourne (died 1826) – marble tablet, surmounted by kneeling female figure (by S. Manning, Senior) and with the deceased's sword mounted beneath it on the north wall of the Brock Chapel; Sir Isaac Brock – white marble tablet on the same wall; Rear-Admiral Thomas Saumarez Brock, his wife and eldest son – marble tablet with coat of arms at the centre (by E. Henry) on the west wall of the south transept; Major-General Sir Octavius Carey – marble

tablet surmounted by coat of arms (by Westminster Marble
Co.) on the south wall of the south transept; Eric d'Auvergne
Collings (died 1916) – marble tablet on the north wall, near
the baptistry, with the wooden cross from his grave in France
on the right-hand side; John Collings (died 1820) and others –
marble tablet surmounted by a funeral urn (by John Bacon,
the Younger) on the west wall of the south transept; Osmond
de Beauvoir (died 1810) – marble tablet surmounted by a
weeping figure and an urn and with a coat of arms at the base
(by J. Bacon, the Younger) on the west wall of the south transept; James Lord de Saumarez (died 1836) – marble tablet
with a coat of arms above, a female figure on either side and a
naval action in progress beneath (by William Whitelaw) on
the south wall of the nave; James Saumarez Dobrée (1801–
59) – marble tablet (by Edward Richardson) on the north wall
of the Brock Chapel; the Very Reverend Daniel Francis
Durand (died 1832) and his wife – marble tablet depicting a
dying husband on a sofa and a grieving wife (by Edward
Hodges Baily, R.A.) on the south wall of the nave; James
Jeremie (died 1844) and his wife – marble tablet (by E.
Richardson) on the west wall of the south transept; Lieutenant Stewart Alexander Kershaw and his wife – marble tablet
(by Baily) on the south wall of the nave; General Hubert Le
Cocq – marble tablet (by Gaffin) with sword mounted
beneath it, on the west wall of the nave; William Le Marchant
(died 1768) and family – marble tablet (by Francis Legatt
Chantrey, R.A.,) on the north wall of the Brock Chapel;
Captain Nicholas Le Messurier (died 1759) commander of the
Guernsey-owned private ship of war *Bellona* of 20 guns –
marble tablet on the south wall of the nave; Catherine de
Carteret (née Lemprière) (died 1610) wife of Amyce de
Carteret, Lieutenant-Governor and Bailiff of Guernsey –
marble tablet with three coats of arms, one above (de Carteret
impaling Lemprière) and one on either side (left de Carteret:
right Lemprière) on the west wall of the south transept; Sir
Edward Chepmell Ozanne (died 1929), Bailiff (1915–22) –
marble tablet on the arch on the south side of the north aisle;
Peter Perchard (died 1806), Lord Mayor of London, and his
wife – white marble tablets on pillar on the south side of the

nave; General Sir Thomas Saumarez (died 1845) – marble tablet surmounted by an urn and a weeping figure (by Baily); Captain William Sheldon, Lieutenant-Governor (died 1680) – marble tablet on a pillar on the south wall of nave; Major-General John Small (died 1796), Lieutenant-Governor – white marble tablet on the south wall of the nave; Colonel Sir George Smith (died 1809) and his wife – marble tablet surmounted by a broken column and a coat of arms (by J. Bacon, the Younger).

The following flags hang in the church: west door, the Queen's and Regimental Colours of the 1st The Royal Guernsey Light Infantry (East or Town Regiment); chancel, the Queen's and the Regimental Colours of The Royal Guernsey Light Infantry (East or Town Regiment) later 1st Battalion The Royal Guernsey Light Infantry (Militia), the King's and Regimental Colours of the 1st Battalion The Royal Guernsey Light Infantry (Militia) later the Royal Guernsey Militia; Brock Chapel, The King's Colour of the 1st Service Battalion The Royal Guernsey Light Infantry, presented at G.H.Q. France on 24 January 1919 by the Chief of the General Staff. Finally, in the church hangs the flag flown on H.M.S. *Alsatian*, flagship of the 10th Cruiser Squadron, under the command of Vice-Admiral Sir Reginald Tupper, K.C.B., C.V.O.

The church plate includes: the Guille Cruet, an exceedingly rare item probably dating from 1530–35, a copy of the same (except for inscription) bearing the London hallmark for 1895, a flagon on the pattern of the Guille Cruet, gilt and bearing the London hallmark for 1846, a chalice probably dating from about 1390, but possibly from as late as 1544, two chalices, an alms dish, and three patens, all gilt and bearing the London hallmark for 1846, a pair of candlesticks bearing the London hallmark for 1894, and a cruet set consisting of two silver jugs for water and wine and a wafer-box. The church also holds in safe keeping the Queen's chalice and paten presented by Queen Elizabeth (now the Queen Mother) for the use of all the churches in Guernsey and Sark to commemorate the royal visit of 1945. Finally, the church possesses a set of four hexagonal brass offertory boxes inscribed and dated 1680.

The church has eight bells, in addition to the clock bell. The first seven bells are inscribed "CORNILLE-HAVARD A VILLEDIEU FRANCE"; the eighth bell (tenor) is inscribed "THIS PEAL OF EIGHT BELLS WAS ERECTED BY PARISHIONERS AND FRIENDS 1913 THOMAS BELL, DEAN. JOHN PERCY DE PUTRON, RECTOR. CHARLES JAMES DURAND JOHN BONAMY COLLINGS CHURCHWARDENS TO THE HONOUR AND GLORY OF GOD AND IN MEMORY OF GEORGE EDWARD LEE RECTOR OF THIS PARISH 1881–1912 CORNILLE-HAVARD A VILLEDIEU FRANCE".

Parish registers start as follows: marriages (1565), burials (1566) and baptisms (1630).

In the north porch there are two carved rabbits, one on either side of the door. Above the porch is a room reached from inside the church by a winding staircase entered from the north transept. There are also two weathered carved heads on the exterior of the church, one on the south-east corner of the south transept and the other on the north-east corner of the Brock Chapel.

On the north wall of the church is a plaque to the memory of Major-General Sir Isaac Brock (1769–1812) presented by the government of Ontario in 1969.

Near the north-east corner of the church, adjacent to Albion House, is one of St Peter Port's ancient barrier stones.

CASTEL CHURCH (St Mary of Castel) stands on an eminence, believed to be the site of an ancient castle, and is one of the most prominent landmarks in Guernsey. It is located at the junction of La Rue du Presbytère and Les Rohais de Haut, Castel.

The church, known to have existed as early as 1155, is stone-vaulted and roofed with slate. It has a tower with a clock in its south wall, an octagonal spire and a spirelet at each corner, centrally situated over the north aisle. Access is gained to the tower from inside the church by means of a wooden staircase. The interior of the church consists of a nave, a north aisle, a chancel and a chapel to the north of the chancel, now used as a vestry. There is a massive arcade between the nave and the north aisle. The groining under the tower is of grey granite and at the base of each of the four vaulting ribs is a shield.

The church is notable for its thirteenth-century wall-paintings high up on the north wall of the chapel to the north of the chancel. They extend for 37 feet from the arch supporting the tower to the east wall of the church. They depict from west to east the "Three Living and the Three Dead", the figure of a man on the flat rib projecting from the wall and the "Last Supper". The first picture depicts a tree with seven branches, three mounted courtiers, each with a falcon, and three corpses in varying stages of decomposition. Two of the courtiers and a horse have expressions of surprise. The second picture depicts a figure of a man wearing a black habit and holding a flagon in his right hand and a chalice in his left. Across his neck is laid an axe. The third picture depicts Jesus and the Twelve Apostles seated at a table on which are cups, plates and knives. In front of the table are two figures. One is possibly a servant placing on the table a dish containing a fish; the other, with long hair, is possibly Mary Magdalene.

The church has a piscina to the right of the altar and a squint in the south-east pillar of the tower.

The credence table and altar on the north side of the church date from 1966. The reredos depicts the Madonna and Child with angels on either side.

The church has what is said to be a low side window. It is filled with stained glass to the memory of Thomas Lenfesty and other members of the family.

The church plate includes: a basin or platter bearing the London hallmark for 1771, a lidded flagon by Pierre Amiraux of Jersey (undated), and a baptismal jug, possibly by a Guernsey maker, with the mark "JH" with a sunburst twice (undated). All the pieces bear inscriptions.

The church has three bells re-cast at the Whitechapel Foundry in 1811. The treble and the second bear the same inscription "THOMAS MEARS OF LONDON FECIT 1811"; the tenor, in addition, bears the names of the rector and church-wardens of the time.

The registers start in 1674.

In the churchyard near the west porch stands a statue menhir dating probably from the second or third century. In front of the figure is the stone seat of the Court of the Manor of St Michael. There is also an old red granite trough carved with two faces, said to represent the sun and the moon, possibly a sixteenth- or seventeenth-century garden trough.

The churchyard also contains the tomb of Admiral Lord de Saumarez, and a grotto.

FOREST CHURCH (St Margaret's), situated at Rue de l'Eglise, Forest, is the smallest ancient parish church in Guernsey, and is known to have existed as early as about 1048. It has a tower above the centre of the south aisle with an octagonal spire and four spirelets. The spire is surmounted by a weathercock. In the tower is a clock paid for by public subscription to commemorate Queen Victoria's Diamond Jubilee in 1897. The interior of the building, which is stone-vaulted, consists of a north aisle with the chancel at the east end and a south aisle.

The church has an ancient poor-box made out of a solid oak log bound with iron. It stands immediately to the right (looking from inside) of the north door and above it on the wall is a plaque stating that it is the *"Boite pour les Pauvres Honteux"* (the proud poor) and bearing the date 1786.

In the glass-fronted case on the north wall to the left (looking from inside) of the north door are preserved instruments – a fife, a piccolo, two flutes and a clarinet – from the old church band which provided music before the days of organs. The organ is located at the east end of the south aisle.

In the chancel, to the right of the altar, is a good example of a piscina. The font is of Finnish granite and was installed in 1968 in memory of the Reverend J.H. Finey by his sisters.

All the windows contain some stained glass. One at the east end depicts St Margaret both as a shepherdess and a virgin martyr.

In the chancel is a marble memorial tablet to the Reverend Edouard Mourant of Jersey, Rector of Forest and Torteval for thirty-nine years until transferred to St Andrew's in 1836, in which year he died.

The church has the following plate: two English-made wine cups (both 1698), a basin or platter (1694), a flagon by Pierre Maingy of Guernsey, given to the church by Nicolas Allez in 1756, a ewer (1789), a plain footed paten by Jean Perchard of Guernsey (undated), a salver or paten on three feet (1778) and a number of recent additions. Most of the pieces bear inscriptions.

The church also has four bells dating respectively from 1685 (two), 1894 and 1896.

The registers date from 1574.

The round-headed doorway of the north entrance is like one would find in an old Guernsey house. The south entrance has a porch.

The entrance to the churchyard on the north side is through a lychgate bearing on its north side the words "PRO PATRIA". The gate was erected as a war memorial by the parish and incorporates tablets to the memory of those who fell in both World Wars.

The church was closed by the Germans during 1940 and re-opened for use in 1941 when one service was held at 3 p.m. each Sunday. The rectory was commandeered as an officers' billet and the rector went to stay at St Martin's.

At the corner of the main road and the road leading to Petit Bôt bay is a stone four feet high inscribed "PERRON DU ROY" which may have formed part of a vanished megalithic structure known as *"Le Trépied des Nouettes"*.

ST ANDREW'S CHURCH (St Andrew of the Sloping Orchard), is situated on the side of a hill on the eastern side of La Rue des Morts where it joins St Andrew's Road.

The church, which is known to have existed in about 1048, is built of granite of a pinkish hue, is stone-vaulted and partially roofed with slates. It has a square tower at the west end of the north aisle with a clock with faces in its south and west sides. The tower has a battlemented parapet and is surmounted by a low slate-covered spire bearing a weathercock. The interior of the building, which is dark owing to the stained-glass windows, comprises a north aisle, a nave and chancel.

The vaulting beneath the tower is groined and there is a

circular opening at the centre.

The carved oak reredos was placed in the church in 1909. The organ was given by the parishioners in memory of Queen Victoria.

The font stands at the west end of the building.

The church has a number of memorials including one to Jean Guille of Rohais who died in 1758, and another to Charles Antoine Frederic Gounon de Pradon (died 1778), the rector whose name appears on the tenor bell.

The church possesses a baptismal jug by a Guernsey maker with the mark "JH" and sunburst twice (undated), two chalices, a flagon, two patens and a spoon (all dated 1859).

The church has three bells all inscribed "PACK & CHAPMAN LONDRES FECIT 1778" with, in the case of the tenor bell, the name of the rector and churchwardens added.

The parish registers are preserved from 1574 with the exception of the years 1599–1603 and 1616–19.

There is a drainhead dated 1805 at the west end of the building.

Near the church is La Fontaine de St Clair.

ST MARTIN OF THE BELLOUSE is built on a mound and is situated at Rue de l'Eglise, St Martin.

The church, which is known to have existed in about 1048, is stone-vaulted and roofed with slates. It has a tower situated above the nave slightly east of centre. The tower has an octagonal granite spire with a spirelet at each corner. In the south face of the tower is a clock. The interior of the building comprises a nave, chancel and north aisle.

Just inside the south door is the pre-Reformation font, the only one in Guernsey, and said to be the original one belonging to the church to which it was restored in 1869.

The church has box pews, and there is internal access to the tower by means of an iron spiral staircase.

Items worth noting are the piscina of Caen stone in the south wall of the chancel adjacent to the altar, the pulpit dated 1657, the poor-box consisting of an oak cupboard with a door carved with a design and bearing the word *"Pauvres"* set into a recess in the wall, formerly a water stoup, on the east side of the south door, and a clarinet from the church band of years gone by.

All the windows contain stained glass. One, in memory of General George de Sausmarez, depicts the angels adoring the risen Christ. Another, the three-light west window, an anonymous memorial – by M.E. de Putron (1957), depicts St Martin with shields bearing the arms of England, Winchester, Coutances, Tours and France on a clear background. The three-light east window displays a Victorian Ascension in memory of Captain Richard Charles McCrea which was re-set in clear glass (1956) by M.E. de Putron. The south window in the chancel (1958 – by Charles Carey) depicts the Holy Family at Nazareth. There is a rose window over the door at the west end.

There are a number of memorials to well-known St Martin's families – Andros, Carey, de Sausmarez and Gosselin. Among them is one to the memory of Amice Andros, Seigneur of Sausmarez, who was Bailiff of Guernsey from 1661 to 1674 and Elizabeth Andros (née Stone), his wife. It is a white marble mural tablet with the arms of de Sausmarez at the top and those of Andros at the bottom.

The church has two chalices and two patens (all dated 1854), a flagon (1853) and a ciborium (1962).

In the tower are three bells re-cast by Jean Baptiste Brocard of Lorraine in 1736. They all bear inscriptions.

The south porch, in the Flamboyant style, is very fine. The corner buttresses are set diagonally and terminate in pinnacles ornamented with crockets and finials. A sundial has replaced the top of the pinnacle above the entrance. Inside the porch there are stone seats.

There is a granite tombstone to the memory of Samuel de la Place, the last but one of the Calvinist Ministers, on the north side of the west door.

At the southern entrance to the churchyard is 'The Grandmother of the Cemetery', a rectangular stone pillar terminating in a carved female head and shoulders, serving as a gatepost between two gates. It probably dates from the sixth century A.D.

ST PETER-IN-THE-WOOD CHURCH is situated at Rue de l'Eglise, St Peter's. John Justice (1350) is the first recorded rector.

The building, which is known to have existed in 1030, has wooden ceilings and is roofed with slates. At its western end it has a tower about 114 feet high with a battlemented parapet and two angle-buttresses, one at the north-west corner and the other at the south-west. The tower is reached from the interior of the church by a spiral stone staircase. The interior of the church comprises a nave, two aisles and a chancel. An unusual feature of the building is that it is built on a slope, and there is a difference of 4 feet 8 inches between the floor level at the east end and that at the west end. The slope is downwards from east to west and the octagonal pillars of the arcade increase in height in the same direction.

The alms-box against the west wall is a replica of the old alms-box stolen in 1959. It is made out of a solid oak log and is fitted with an iron top.

There is a round window over the door in the north aisle.

The oak eagle lectern was purchased by the parishioners to commemorate the centenary (1903) of the Brock family holding the incumbency – Thomas Brock (1803–50), Carey Brock (1850–92) and Henry Walter Brock (1892–1918).

The organ is at the west end of the south aisle.

There is a piscina in the south wall of the chancel adjacent to the altar. There are also two oil lamps in the chancel, one in the north-east corner and one in the south-east corner. They are the sole survivors in the church of the fifty-seven lamps which were used to light the building before the installation of electricity in 1929. There are two boards, one on the north wall of the chancel and one on the south wall. On the former are written the Ten Commandments and on the latter the Lord's Prayer and Creed, in both cases in French.

The church has only three stained-glass windows: the three-light east window and the small round-headed window on the south side of the chancel (1870) given jointly by William Pierre Métivier, Jurat, in memory of his wife, Julie Anne, and by the family of Thomas Priaulx in memory of his daughter Louise, who was Julie Anne's sister, and the small round-headed window in full colour depicting St Peter wearing a guernsey and pulling in a fishing net (1972 – by M.E. de Putron) on the north side of the chancel in memory of Canon S.W. Gerhold, Rector from 1947 to 1969.

In the chancel hang the colours of the Fourth Regiment of the Royal Guernsey Militia, as well as the flag of the West British Legion.

At the east end of the north wall of the church is a mural tablet to James Perchard, a Gentleman of the Privy Council of Queen Anne and King George I, in recognition of his gift of £1,000 for the *"Fonds aux Pauvres de la Paroisse"*. He was the son of Jean Perchard, Captain of the Parish Company of Militia, who died in 1697, and grandson of Jean Perchard, minister of the church from 1607 to 1653. There are two other memorials on the same wall to the Reverend Thomas Brock and to Marie Brock (née Carey), his wife.

The church's collection of silver and copper comprises two chalices (1781), a flagon (1831) by William Bateman, a paten with foot (1696), a wafer box (undated), an alms-dish (1696), and two sixteenth-century copper alms-boxes. All the silver pieces are inscribed.

The church has three bells dating respectively from the fifteenth century, 1681 and 1828. The oldest bell was cast at Exeter and bears a Latin inscription. The other two were cast at Villedieu, the older by Paul Bourdon and the more recent by Marquet and bears French inscriptions.

The parish registers of baptisms and marriages were started in February 1628, but they were not regularly kept until 1653, when the registers of burials begin.

There are two entrances on the north side of the church, the tower doorway with its porch and the north aisle doorway, immediately to its east. The tower entrance has an iron-studded door which is very old and made of oak.

There is a gargoyle in the form of a dog's head with long ears on the west wall, south of the tower.

The original altar stone with its five consecration crosses, removed at the Reformation and used as a tombstone into which were let monumental brasses, is preserved in the inner porch of the tower.

In the churchyard are two interesting gravestones, possibly

the oldest in the island. The first records Jean Perchard, Minister 1607–53, an ancestor of Peter Perchard, Lord Mayor of London; the second, close by, commemorates Thomas de Lisle who left a silver cup to the church under his will dated 1629.

Outside the north church gates is a granite mounting block.

The parish war memorial, in granite, stands on Les Buttes, part of the old parochial archery ground, to the east of the church. At the top end of Les Buttes stands the parish hall, once the day school, where the Douzaine meet.

The rectory stands to the south of the churchyard on a site where a previous rectory was built in 1441.

ST SAMPSON'S CHURCH is in the New Road near the South Quay of St Sampson's Harbour. The first recorded rector is Leonard Le Conte. The living was separated from that of Vale in 1859.

The church, which is known to have existed in about 1048, is stone-vaulted except for the south aisle and roofed with slates. It has a saddleback tower on the north side about midway along the length of the building. It comprises a nave, chancel and two chapels, one on the north side, dedicated to St Maglorius in 1973, and one on the south side (not used as a chapel), with a vestry extending from the south-east chapel.

The building contains two piscinae, one of Caen stone to the right of the altar and the other at the east end of the south aisle. The font stands beneath the tower and was given in memory of Alfred Thomas Kennedy (1851–55). The brass lectern was given in memory of Frederick Reginald Leale, killed in 1916. There is good woodwork in the chancel. The sanctuary chairs are of the Glastonbury design. In the north wall of St Maglorius's Chapel are three recesses, the centre one of which has a long cross deeply cut into the stone and is almost certainly a tomb. The two houseling stools (which may be used either as seats or communion rails) in the same chapel were presented in memory of Frederick, Florence and Rex Coysh.

The church has the following plate: a chalice of parcel gilt (about 1525), a bell-shaped chalice on turned baluster stem with parcel gilt interior with maker's mark "IS" and a coronet twice, ewer (probably a domestic cream jug) (1800), four Sheffield plate dishes, two oval and two round, one on four feet, a flagon, two dishes with feet, an oval dish (1816), two cups (1815), a shaped circular piecrust tray on triple collet feet by Guillaume Henry of Guernsey, and a plated paten.

In addition, the church owns a collection of English made latten dating from between 1500 and 1520 found hidden in the tower on 20 June 1913. The collection comprises a cross and base, a censer bowl, a standing candlestick, a standing candlestick on three lion's feet, triple candlestick (one branch missing), three brackets, one in the shape of a serpent, one in the shape of a dragon and one plain, and a loose bowl and pricket. These items have been incorporated into St Maglorius's Chapel and the baptistry.

All the windows contain stained glass. The three-light east window (by Hardman) over the altar depicting "The Resurrection" is to the memory of Martha Amelia Ozanne (née Chepmell), wife of John Ozanne. The two-light east window (by Clayton and Bell) in St Maglorius's Chapel depicting Dorcas distributing to the poor is to the memory of Lady Giffard. The round-headed window on the north side of the tower depicting Christ blessing little children is to the memory of Elizabeth Chepmell. The two-light east window (by Clayton and Bell) in the South Chapel depicting St Peter's attempt to walk on the water is to the memory of Agnew Giffard and Walter John Giffard. The two-light window in the south wall of the same chapel depicting the Virgin Mary and St John (1891) is to the memory of John Abraham Lainé and Louisa Lainé (née Moullin), his wife. The small west window (by Shrigley and Hunt) depicts St Sampson. The small window in the south wall (by Shrigley and Hunt) depicting St Peter is to the memory of the Reverend G.C. Whalley, a former curate of the parish. There is a window in the nave depicting Charity to the memory of Mrs G.F. Peek. The window over the gallery is to the memory of the Reverend Robert Jones, Rector (1892–1909). There are two windows (1933) in the north side of the chancel depicting respectively "The Good Shepherd" and "The Good

Samaritan", the latter to the memory of John Blight. There are two windows in the north side of the nave depicting respectively the Madonna and Child and Christ teaching a child, the former to the memory of Sir Gerald Giffard and the latter to the memory of Sir Henry Giffard and his son Walter Giffard. Finally, there is a window (1970 – by M.E. de Putron) in the south side of the porch depicting St Sampson standing before the west front of St Sampson's Church to the memory of Canon Edward Louis Frossard, Rector of St Sampson (1918–58; Dean of Guernsey 1947–67) and Margery Smith Frossard (née Latta), his wife.

The memorials are particularly worth noting. The first, over the priest's stall in the chancel, is a tablet to two persons one of whom was Thomas Falla, a lieutenant in the 12th Regiment of Infantry, who died at the Siege of Seringapatam on 6 April 1799 of a wound from a solid cannon ball weighing 26 pounds, which became lodged between the two bones of one of his thighs and remained undetected until after his death, despite the examination of the wound by the regimental surgeon. A remarkable story, but for all that largely corroborated from contemporary sources. The second, in the South Chapel, near the vestry door, is to Cecil Lerrier Giffard, an officer of the 11th North Regiment who was killed at Maidan, Northern India, during the Tirah campaign. Beneath the memorial hangs the deceased's sword. There is also a memorial to Eleazer Le Marchant, Jurat, 1703.

In the chancel hang the colours of the North Regiment of the Royal Guernsey Militia.

The church has one bell in the tower and another in a niche above the door of the north aisle. The former bearing a long inscription was re-cast by Nicholas Blondel, a Guernseyman, in 1759; the latter probably dates from the second half of the nineteenth century.

Exterior features of the building worth noting are the indentations known as corbie steps in the coping of the gable of the main west front and that of the west front of the north chapel, the niche over the north door and the sundial which is the bottom stone of the gable on the southern corner of the nave. It is the top stone at the west when viewed from the southern side.

Alongside the path close to the west entrance are two grave-stones. The one nearer the door bears the initials "M L D V" and a date probably either 1628 or 1638; the one farther from the door bears the date 1619.

At the north-east corner of the churchyard facing the road is a public fountain dated 1896.

ST SAVIOUR'S CHURCH is situated at Rue de l'Eglise, St Saviour. It is known to have existed as early as 1030, and its first recorded rector is Simon de St Martin (1309).

The church, which is the largest outside St Peter Port, is stone-vaulted and roofed with slates. It has a tower at the west end of the north aisle with a battlemented parapet and an octagonal lead-covered spire surmounted by a weathercock. The tower has an angle buttress at its north-west corner and a buttress at the southern end of its west side. Each buttress is in two stages and terminates in a triangular head with flowers at the apex. In the east face of the tower is a clock installed in 1968. The belfry is reached from within the church by a spiral stone staircase the exterior of which slightly protrudes from the north wall of the tower. The Germans used the tower as an observation post during the Occupation. The interior of the church comprises a nave, a north aisle, the Bethlehem Chapel giving off the nave and a sacristy (1960) in a small building at the east end of the north aisle.

The pillars between the nave and the north aisle are of two distinct types, circular and octagonal. At the base of the four ribs of the groining of the belfry are raised pieces of stone which, on the north-east and south-west corners are in the shape of a shield. The former is plain but the latter has some lettering on it, as yet undeciphered. A wrought-iron grille divides the nave from the Bethlehem Chapel on its south side.

There is an alms-box made out of an oak log, with two big padlocks, dating from the seventeenth century at the west end of the church. The font, which was brought from St Peter Port Church in 1886, is located beneath the tower as are two of the old bell-clappers. A display case in the south-west corner of the nave contains interesting items belonging to the church. Some of the pews have doors. The wooden lectern was carved by James Alexandre, a Jerseyman. The altar came from St Barnabas's Church. The altar in the Chapel of the Passion in the north aisle came from St James's Church.

The church has seven stained-glass windows: a small one towards the east end of the north aisle, the magnificent east window (1956), four on the south side of the nave, two to the east and two to the west of the chapel including one depicting the Virgin Mary and the infant Jesus accepting from the Magi gifts of gold, frankincense and myrrh to the memory of Alice Carey, the daughter of Pierre Carey, a former rector, and one at the west end of the north aisle.

The church plate includes: two chalices (1698), two plates or patens, a ewer, a flagon (1734), a silver-plated altar set comprising a cross, two candlesticks, two vases and a missal stand to match, and a silver wafer box given in memory of the Reverend E.F. Wood (Rector 1931–53). The church also possesses an unusual set of two leather collecting mugs dating from 1813.

The church possesses three bells, two dating from 1680, cast by Paul Bourdon, and the third from 1856, re-cast by Viel Tetrel, all bearing inscriptions.

The parish registers date from 1582 but are incomplete for the first thirty years. The oldest known copy of *La Dédicace des Eglises* is in the Register of Marriages and Baptisms (No. 3).

The doorway towards the west end of the north side of the church is like an old Guernsey dwelling house doorway. On the north side of the tower, about three feet above ground, there is a stone with a cross on it. While over the doorway of the porch on the south side of the church is a sundial.

At the east entrance to the churchyard is a large stone, probably a Christianized menhir, with a deeply incised cross on its front and a smaller one on its back, both centrally placed.

A stone bench at the top of the steps at the end of the path running from Sous l'Eglise to the church is the meeting-place of the Court of the Manor of Jean du Gailliard.

Two large stone slabs at ground level between the south porch of the church and the boiler house covered the graves of

British soldiers quartered at Fort Richmond who died during the Napoleonic Wars.

A slate gravestone standing near the south-east boundary of the churchyard marks the grave of eleven Irish men and women, passengers of the cutter *Pitt* bound from Jersey to Falmouth wrecked on the rocks between L'Erée and Richmond on 26 November 1819.

The oldest gravestone in the churchyard is that of Nicholas Torode who died in 1602. Another ancient gravestone is that to the memory of Jean Perchard who died in 1653 aged 72 years after 47 years in the ministry. He was ancestor to Peter Perchard, Lord Mayor of London (1804–5). A more recent gravestone bears just two words *"Ma Mère"*.

TORTEVAL CHURCH, Rue de la Belle, Torteval, is dedicated to St Philip although the church which it replaced was originally dedicated to the Virgin Mary.

Old Torteval Church is known to have existed as long ago as about 1048. The present building by John Wilson dates from 1816 in which year the foundation stone was laid by Lieutenant-General Sir John Doyle, the Lieutenant-Governor.

The church is built of grey granite and has a circular battlemented tower at its west end with a circular spire surmounted by a weathervane dated 1774. It has an apsidal east end.

The interior of the building is simple. The organ is in the gallery at the west end of the nave. Although electricity is used for lighting, the old bracket oil lamps are preserved. The font of Irish marble came from St Barnabas's Church to which it was presented by the Meyrick family as a memorial to Miss Christina Anne Guille. There is only one memorial.

Above the altar is a stained-glass window (1958) depicting Christ meeting with St Philip "Hast thou not known me, Philip?" presented as a thanks-offering for the Liberation.

The church has a paten bearing the Guernsey maker's mark "IH" and a sunburst once in a dish presented in 1727, two identical chalices (1831), a flagon (1832), an alms-dish (1832), all except the first bear an inscription surmounted by the Le Marchant Arms.

The church also has three bells dating respectively from 1432, 1843 and 1881. The first is almost certainly French, the second was re-cast by C. Martin of Guernsey and the third was cast by A. Havard of Villedieu and is said to have come from St Barnabas's Church.

The parish registers start in the late seventeenth century.

The crenellated granite porch was added in 1883.

At the west end of the churchyard is the grey granite war memorial. Adjoining the east end is a bird sanctuary (1977) established to commemorate the Silver Jubilee of Queen Elizabeth II.

VALE CHURCH (St Michael of the Vale) stands on an elevated site bordering L'Ancresse Road, Vale. Until the reclamation of La Braye du Valle in 1806 the church was cut off from the island at high tide and worshippers had to use boats in order to attend services. The parish was united with that of St Sampson from 1607 until 1859. Robert, Priest and Dean of the Vale (1156), is the first recorded Prior of the Vale and Jean Le Carpentier (1473) is the first recorded Rector of the Vale.

The church, which is known to have existed as early as 1155, is stone-vaulted and roofed with slates. It has a tower above the south-west corner of the nave with an octagonal spire covered with brown cement and surmounted by a weathercock. At each corner of the tower is a spirelet. There is a clock with four faces let into the spire. The interior of the church consists of a nave, a nave aisle, a chancel, the Chapel of the Archangels to the north of the chancel, and a vestry on the north side of the chapel.

Three of the pillars of the arcade dividing the nave from the nave aisle bear corbels on their west sides a little distance below the capitals. The most westerly depicts a lion's head, the other two are defaced. On the arch above the pulpit is a carving of a dog's head (probably a spaniel's). The east window of the chapel retains its original tracery.

Undoubtedly the chancel is the most interesting part of the church. It has a groined roof, but owing to a serious settlement the ribs of the vaulting above the bay closest to the chancel arch are out of alignment and the top of the chancel arch is considerably depressed. The mosaic reredos was erected in 1904 as a token of esteem for the Rector, Thomas Bell, to mark his fiftieth anniversary as rector. He was to continue in office for a further ten years. On the right of the altar is a piscina, one of three in the church. The other two are located in the south wall of the south aisle near the chancel arch and in the Chapel of the Archangels respectively. The piscina in the chapel is of granite. There is a sedilia comprising seven seats on the same level on the south side of the chancel.

There is a stained-glass window over the altar to the memory of J.H. Ingrouille. During the Occupation he was sentenced by the Germans to five years imprisonment of which he served four years in various prisons, the last being Brandenberg, Germany. He was found by a British Army Officer and sent to hospital in Brussels where he died on 13 June 1945. The following year his body was brought to Guernsey and buried in Domaille Cemetery at Vale Church. On the north side is a window in full colour (1978 – by M.E. de Putron) depicting Christ knocking at the door of the human soul in memory of Albert E. Guilbert and Emilie Guilbert (née Le Poidevin), his wife. On the south side is another window in full colour (1974 – by M.E. de Putron) depicting Christ and fishermen in memory of Charles Rew. There is also a window in memory of Alfred John Robin and Edith Elizabeth Robin (née Henry), his wife. The west window (1977) in the baptistry is in memory of Mildred Alice Renouf.

There is a memorial slab in the Chapel of the Archangels bearing the inscription *"Orate pro anima Galfridi"*, and in the paving on the west side of the screen dividing the chapel from the nave aisle is a stone into which memorial brasses were once set. There were evidently two figures, one of a man and one of a woman, and a shield.

The church plate includes: a chalice (1890), a flagon (1936), a ciborium (1966), and a chalice, a ciborium and a wafer box (all post 1967).

The belfry contains bells all dating from 1891 and inscribed.

The parish registers are preserved as follows: baptisms and marriages from 1577; burials from 1604. The entries were made in French until 1939.

Inside the north porch over the door is a niche which no doubt once contained a statue, and there are unusual canopies over three windows on the north side.

Near the south-west corner of the church is a seventh- or eighth-century tombstone discovered in January 1949 buried outside the west door.

ST ANNE'S CHURCH (Old), Le Huret, St Anne, Alderney, was replaced by a new church with the same dedication, and all that remains of the old church is the tower now called the 'clock tower' and the churchyard.

The decision to erect the tower and a chapel with a porch on the north side of the church was taken on 28 September 1761, but the clock tower was not built until 1767.

The tower is constructed of stone and has a conical spire, surmounted by a weathervane, and four spirelets. Beneath the clock is a sundial.

According to Sharpe, the tower contains two bells, the smaller inscribed "CLEMANT TOSEAR CAST MEE IN 1701" and almost certainly cast at Salisbury, and the larger inscribed "J LE MESURIER PRAEFECT T LE COCQ AEDIT ANNO DOMINI 1760".

3

The Ancient Chapels of Jersey, Guernsey and Herm

THE FISHERMEN'S CHAPEL stands in the churchyard of St Brelade's Church to the south of the church from which it is only separated by a few feet. The building is stone-vaulted and roofed with slates. At the apex of the east gable is what appears to be a somewhat weathered cross but is supposed to represent a monk in his habit. The chapel has one entrance at the west end of the north wall. The stone altar with its five consecration crosses came from Mont Orgueil Castle into whose fabric it had been built after the Reformation. The five windows are filled with glass by Bosdet, the subjects being: north window, "St Brendan's Boat among the Icebergs"; west window, "St Brendan's Landing in Jersey and a local Chieftain embracing Christianity"; west window, south side, "St Brendan as a Student"; east window, south side, "St Brendan holding a Thanksgiving Service on the Isle of Birds"; east window, "The Youth of St Brelade".

The chapel is ancient but exactly how old it is no one knows and it is not known to whom it was dedicated. Before the Reformation it must have presented a splendid sight with its plastered walls and vault covered with wall-paintings. After the Reformation it had a chequered history and at one time was used as an armoury.

William Plees writing in 1817 described the chapel at some length:

> This chapel is supposed to have taken its name from the number of fishermen residing in the neighbourhood, fish constituting the principal traffic of its inhabitants. The rectors, if then so called, of all the parishes in Jersey enjoyed at that time a tithe of fish: this is still their right; but from the difficulties and altercations an enforcement would occasion, it is no longer

claimed. Another account of the chapel is, that it was frequent-
ly the resort of Norman fishermen, who had a priest residing
near it to perform the ministerial offices; one either selected by
themselves, or delegated from the see of Coutances, and who
might possibly receive his emoluments, wholly or partly, in
fish caught by the strangers, or from the produce of what they
sold to the natives in the vicinity, or bartered with them: the
former of these traditions seems to be the most probable
account.

'The interior of the chapel has been ornamented with a
variety of figures, displaying different scenes from the New
Testament. These figures are about four feet in height, and
painted in colours on the plastered walls; but time, accident,
and perhaps wantonness, have nearly effaced them. On the
right is still distinguishable an angel, having in one hand a
label, on which is an inscription in Gothic characters. He holds
this towards a female, whose hands are uplifted in the attitude
of praying: behind her, on a curvated pole, is a reading desk,
with a book open, in which are some nearly illegible letters. We
may venture to suppose this to represent the annunciation. On
the left-hand wall is a man, crowned, with an antique sword in
his right hand: from his mouth issues a scroll, on which is
inscribed, *herod le roy*. His garments are of an olive colour, and
over them is a scarlet robe flowing to the ground. On the lower
part of the same wall is Jesus Christ, bearing the cross, depicted with yellowish hair, and his head surrounded with a glory.
Over the entrance, which is opposite to the west, is the figure
of a man, robed, with a number of naked persons round him;
some at full length, others just emerging from the ground.
This is doubtless a representation of the general resurrection.
The figures of this composition are smaller than those on the
side walls. All are tolerably well proportioned; but, like many
other ancient religious portraits, there is little expression in the
features of those personages. The figures are mere sketches;
but the colours appear to be well preserved. The chapel is now
employed as an armory for the parochial artillery, so that the
whole of those antique designs cannot be seen, unless when the
guns &c. are drawn out;

Writing in 1859, J.N.R. de la Croix in his book *Jersey: Ses
Antiquités, Ses Institutions, Son Histoire. Volume I* also gives
a detailed description of the chapel.

Today at the east end of the chapel on the vault and on the
north and south side walls is a painting of *The Annunciation*,

heavily re-painted when it was discovered about 1915–18 beneath another painting said to be of *The Assumption*, which was removed. This painting now runs into the paintings on the side walls and at one time extended lower than it does at present. It depicts at the apex God the Father with rays extending down to the Virgin Mary, who, with the Angel Gabriel, occupies the centre of the picture. On the right there is a building, and a lectern with a book on it on which rests one of the Virgin's hands. At the base the composition is flanked on the left by seven kneeling males, and on the right by a similar number of kneeling females, no doubt benefactors of the chapel. The painting has a 'bent ribbon' border all around it; below the border at the base is a black and white quatrefoil border. The south-east wall within the chancel area is covered with Old Testament scenes. The wall to the west appears to have had a Nativity series. The north wall has a Passion series in two sequences, one above the other, the upper sequence from east to west and the lower sequence from west to east. The west wall has a version of *The Last Judgment* with Christ seated in majesty above and *The General Resurrection* below. One set of paintings probably dates from the fourteenth century and the other from the second quarter of the fifteenth century.

THE CHAPEL OF OUR LADY OF THE DAWN and the Jerusalem Chapel stand on the summit of La Hougue Bie, Grouville, Jersey. The east end of the former abuts the west end of the latter and they share a tiled roof with a belfry located above the east end of the Chapel of Our Lady of the Dawn. At the apex of the roof at the west end of that chapel is an ancient stone cross found during the course of restoration. Beneath the Jerusalem Chapel is a crypt where at one time there was a representation of the Holy Sepulchre. Both chapels were restored 1924–25.

The Chapel of Our Lady of the Dawn dates possibly from the twelfth century or even earlier. It is stone-vaulted, has two entrances, one on the north side and one on the south, and three windows, one in the west gable and two small and round-headed, one in the north wall and one in the south, in both cases towards the east end. The one on the north side is larger than the one on the south.

THE JERUSALEM CHAPEL which has curved north and south walls dates from early in the sixteenth century. It too is stone-vaulted, has two entrances facing each other, one on the north side and one on the south, with a small window above each, and a window in the east wall. The reason for the two doors being placed opposite one another was probably to have enabled pilgrims viewing holy relics displayed on or in front of the altar to enter by one door and leave by the other, thus avoiding congestion. There is a recess in each of the north, south and east walls. There are two fifteenth-century or very early sixteenth-century paintings of archangels at the east end of the chapel, one on the north vaulting and the other on the south vaulting. Each archangel bears a scroll to which he points. The paintings originally flanked a statue which stood on a bracket between them. Above the statue, at the apex of the vault, were painted what were possibly rays. It has been suggested that the paintings and the statue may have represented the Assumption. The paintings were restored in 1973.

ROZEL MANOR CHAPEL, as its name suggests, is located in the grounds of Rozel Manor, St Martin, Jersey. There is doubt as to its dedication. Some believe that it is dedicated to St Anne, de la Croix records that it is dedicated to St Mary, which is probably the case, and the fact that the manor-house stands on St Marguerite's Hill indicates a third possibility. The building, which is known to have existed at least as early as 1461, is constructed of granite and roofed with tiles. At the apex of the east gable is a cross and at that of the west gable is an open belfry. The imposing west entrance is not original. For the most part the windows are very narrow and round-headed. The austereness of the interior is relieved by the oak choir stalls, carved with saints, including St Bartholomew, St John, St Peter and St Thomas, and dating from about 1600. The west window contains stained glass, after a design by Charles Winston (1814–64) composed of three medallions, one above the other, depicting "The Sermon on the Mount" (top), "Christ Blessing Little Children" (centre), and "Christ Washing the Disciples' Feet", dedicated to the memory of Philip Raoul Lemprière, Lord of the Manor, who died in 1859 and was responsible for the restoration of the building in 1844. The chapel also contains a memorial to Michael Lemprière Bolitho, a captain in the Coldstream Guards, killed in action in 1942.

ST HELIER'S HERMITAGE is built on the side of a rock to the south of Elizabeth Castle, Jersey. At one time the rock was separated from the islet on which the castle stands but now it is connected to it by the breakwater.

It is almost certain that the hermitage was built by the monks of St Helier's Abbey shortly after its foundation in 1155. It takes the form of a chapel, stone-vaulted and roofed with masonry, without slates or tiles. The entrance is in the gable facing the top of the stone stairway providing access from the breakwater, and there is one small window in the opposite gable. In the south wall, close to the south-east corner, is a primitive piscina. The north wall is partly formed of natural rock in which is the cavity known as 'St Helier's Bed'.

On or near St Helier's Day, 16 July, there is a pilgrimage to the hermitage – an event started in 1923.

ST GEORGE'S CHAPEL, Middle Ward, Mont Orgueil Castle, St Martin, Jersey. There is no doubt that the castle had two chapels, St George's and St Mary's. An entry in the Close Rolls for 28 August 1294 records that the King appointed Nicolas Evêque to the Chapel of St Mary and Nicolas Choffyn to the chapel of the fortress (St George's). While in the accounts of Sir John de Roches for 1329 are entered payments made to the two chaplains of the castle. Furthermore, it is known that prior to the Reformation a pilgrimage was made by the islanders to St George's Chapel each year on St George's Day, 23 April. In *The Estate and Orders Militarye of the Castle 1562* there is a reference to "The Chapel Tower, with bell"; in Sir John Peyton's *Book of Repairs to the Castle* there is a reference to "The Chapple and houses adjoining";

and in 1634–37 in the *Accounts for Repairs at the Castle* there is a reference to the Governor's Chapel.

At the Reformation the chapels no doubt suffered in the same way as the other churches and chapels in the island, but probably continued to be used as places of worship. However, the castle was superseded as the principal fortress of the island when Elizabeth Castle was built and was in large measure neglected, although never entirely abandoned as a fortification and from time to time underwent additions, modifications and repairs. In particular, when Admiral Philip d'Auvergne used the castle as his headquarters (1793–1812) parts of the building were renovated for his use.

In 1838 was published *Some Account of Mont Orgueil Castle in the Island of Jersey, etc.* by an anonymous author. In fact, the author was Lieutenant-Colonel Oldfield, K.H., Commanding Royal Engineers.

It is clear from the *Account* that the castle was in a sorry state and that the location of the two chapels had been lost sight of. However, it would seem perfectly clear that the two crypts at present existing are those of St George's and St Mary's. The fact that the coffins of Thomas Overay, Governor (1497–1500), and Sir Anthony Ughtred, Governor (1532–34), were found in 1834 in the lower crypt must surely confirm that it is indeed the crypt of one of the chapels, and in the light of Philip Falle's statement in his *Account of the Island of Jersey* (1734) that the two governors were buried in St George's Chapel, there would appear to be no doubt that the crypt in the lower ward is that of St George's Chapel.

St George's Chapel is described at some length in Oldfield's *Account* as follows:

> The crypt is fifty six feet, eight inches in length, eighteen in breadth; the roof formed of intersecting arches, is eight feet from the floor to the crown of the arch, these arches are composed of small stones, and are about fourteen inches thick: of the four piers which supported the arched roof, two are perfect, these are round, massive and columnar, nearly three diameters in height, they are in all respects similar to the Norman piers described by Rickman, at page 49, of his valuable work upon the different styles of English architecture.

The wall of the crypt, towards the lower Ballium, is five feet thick; the opposite wall, which is next the keep, is three feet six inches, both the side walls of the crypt are supported or strengthened by buttresses; the wall nearest to Le Mont Tower is three feet, and the opposite wall only two feet six; at the north-west end are two openings for windows, blocked up by an accumulation of rubbish; between the wall of the crypt and that of the keep, it seems more than probable there was a passage into which these windows opened, and from which they received light; these, as well as the other three windows in the crypt, appear by the holes in the heads and sills to have been once secured by iron bars of the dimensions of the openings, for the window frames are two feet two inches, and one foot three inches; the jambs having a very considerable splay towards the interior of the crypt; at the opposite end of the crypt, there is an opening for one window, and on the south east side for two windows; on the north west side little of the original wall remains; what openings there may have been, it is difficult to say; in two places there is some appearance of door or window jambs; the space on this side between the crypt, and the passage leading from the fourth gate to the interior of the castle, is so full of cross walls and rubbish, that until these are removed, little more can be ascertained. The walls of the crypt have been plastered, as also the sides of the window openings. A small room has been taken out of the crypt at the south west end; it is nine feet long, and three feet nine inches wide; the vaulted roof of the crypt, which extended over it, has fallen in; there are indications of a window looking towards the lower ward, and the entrance is under a low arch, which most probably was the former doorway of the crypt; this vault or room does not appear to have had any communication with the crypt after it was taken out of it; the walls were plastered; the rubbish has been recently removed, and a temporary roof placed over it. The original appropriation of this vault must be a matter of conjecture, but it seems highly probable it might have been the burying place of the governors.

It would seem that either little was known or remembered as to the existence of this crypt, or that it was altogether disregarded until 1835, when a small part of the roof giving way, boys and others crept in at the opening, bringing down portions of the arch, and the rubbish that covered it. In an attempt to remove the rubbish which had fallen in, three-fifths of the vaulted roof was brought down, and left the crypt in the state in which I first saw it, in January, 1836. The circumstances attending the discovery of the crypt, and the falling in of the roof, were detailed to me by an artilleryman who had been quartered in the castle, and afterwards placed in charge of it by Sir Hilgrove Turner: this man's account was corroborated by the clerk of works in the Engineer Department. In some very interesting notes, published by Mr. Rafter, editor of *The Jersey Times*, mention is made of the recent discovery of the crypt, amongst a mass of ruins overgrown with weeds.

There is no decided appearance of any entrance to the crypt except by the doorway, which was cut off when the vault was made. On the top of the crypt wall are indications of a large window looking towards the lower ward, and on the side of Le Mont Tower there are two door jambs, and steps descending from them in the direction of the tower, the space between which and the crypt is covered with weeds. About the centre of each side wall is a recess, over which there may possibly have been a window: the bottoms of these recesses are paved with three slates like a tessalated pavement, the border slates five inches by three, ˄nd the centre slates diamond fashion, three inches in diameter; the recesses are two feet one inch in length, and one foot four inches in breadth.

A communication is said to have existed between the upper and lower crypts, but of this communication I have as yet been unable to discover the slightest trace.

No record can be found to point out the site of St. George's Chapel, but there appears every probability that it was immediately over the lower crypt.

The earliest known view of the interior of the crypt appears in P.J. Ouless' *Jersey Illustrated*. It depicts the west end of the building and the broken statue of the Virgin Mary referred to later. It also shows two windows with lattice glazing.

Between 1908 and 1921 restoration work was carried out on the chapel. The fallen part of the vaulting in the crypt was replaced. The jambs of the west window of the chapel were partially restored and the stone floor of the chapel was taken up and relaid. Two altar stones, utilized as landings, were installed in 1915, one in the chapel and one in the crypt. A small octagonal pillar was unearthed in the crypt and, as it was believed that it formed one of the original altar pillars, it was re-erected when the altar slab was installed. It is the pillar on the left-hand side. To the left of the altar the natural rock protrudes through the floor to some considerable extent. Behind the altar is a small rectangular window which is blocked up, and appears to be the same as that depicted in de la Croix's *Antiquités* Volume I, page 182.

To-day, the crypt has five windows in addition to the one over the altar, two in the seaward wall, two in the wall facing the middle ward and one in the wall towards Gorey Harbour. None of these windows is glazed.

Entry into the crypt is effected through a doorway placed between the two windows in the wall facing the middle ward. This doorway which is a reconstruction, has a semi-circular arch composed of two concentric rows of voussoirs. The bases of the jambs of the doorway are original.

As has already been stated, before the Reformation there was an annual pilgrimage to St George's Chapel on 23 April. So many took part that at one time the authorities became alarmed lest the castle be overwhelmed and taken by the crowd.

ST MARY'S CHAPEL, Mont Orgueil Castle. The crypt of St Mary's Chapel is described in Oldfield's *Account* as follows:

> The upper crypt is forty-four feet by twenty, and eight feet high to the crown of the arch; the entrance to the crypt, and its communication with the artillery store, have been already mentioned. Towards the sea are two large and one small window; its vaulted roof corresponds in character with that of the lower crypt; it is supported by three piers, two of which are built round, so that they cannot well be seen; the third is columnar, and of the decided Norman character. At the north-east end of this crypt, a mass of masonry has been built up to support the arch; this mass was opened in the spring of 1837, to ascertain if anything was enclosed within it; the arch, composed of small stones of a description similar to that of the vaulted roof of the lower crypt, being found in a dilapidated state, the masonry that had been taken down was immediately replaced.

There are two deeply splayed windows in the seaward wall of the crypt, and a steep stone staircase descends from a doorway in the inner wall to a room (artillery store) at a lower level which forms the basement of the newer keep and has three windows, widely splayed upwards and downwards, overlooking Gorey Harbour.

Above the crypt is St Mary's Chapel, which has a stone-vaulted roof and three windows on the seaward side, the centre one of which is very narrow and deeply splayed. It is described in Oldfield's *Account* thus:

> . . . over the upper crypt is a large vaulted apartment, 44 by 20 feet, and 18 feet in height, the arch is of that description designated by Architects, as a drop arch, (See Plate V, Page 114, of Rickman's English Architecture, 4th edit. 1835), with something like a belfry in the centre, besides the arched door way of cut stone opening into the room from the interior of the keep, there are two other doorways or windows on the same side; and on the opposite side, two full sized Norman windows, and a small window looking towards the sea, at the south-west end a fire place, with an oven, and other conveniences, were made for the use of the troops, when the room was fitted up as barracks for sixty men in the year 1778, the order for the execution of this service, mentions the room as "a damaged vaulted antic place". The bedsteads, and other fitments placed in it, by this order, were only removed in 1834.

The *Account* also includes a description of the statue of the Virgin Mary which was found by Oldfield in the castle as follows:

> Since these sheets have been in the press, in the north wall of this court, embedded in the masonry, an image of the Virgin has been discovered, wrought in what is pronounced by an experienced statuary to be a coarse description of Portland Stone. The head is broken off, from the feet to the shoulders, the height is four feet four inches, the Virgin is holding in her arms the infant Jesus; this figure has been much mutilated. The image of the virgin has been coloured and gilt, and notwithstanding the coarseness of the material, the sculpture is good.

This statue is now on display in the Castle Museum with a brass plate above it giving particulars of its discovery. It is depicted in some detail in de la Croix's *Antiquités* Volume I, page 268.

In the early 1930s a piece of another statue, a hand grasping a staff, was found at the foot of Prynne's Tower.

It should also be mentioned that some of the shields displaying the cross of St George inserted around the top of the Somerset Tower were carved out of religious statuary.

There is nothing to indicate whether the religious statuary referred to above came from the castle's chapels or from elsewhere.

ST MARY'S PRIORY was built on Maître Ile, Les Ecréhous, St Martin, Jersey, in the first half of the thirteenth century and comprised a chapel and living quarters.

In 1203 Piers des Préaux, Lord of the Channel Islands, under King John of England, from 1200 to 1206, gave by charter to the Abbey of St Mary of Val Richer in Normandy the whole of Les Ecréhous for the salvation of the King's soul, as well as those of himself, his father and mother and of all his ancestors, as a site for a church to be built to the honour of God and the blessed Mary.

In *Quo Warranto* proceedings before the King's Justices in Eyre held in 1309 the prior stated that he, another monk and a servant lived in the priory and kept a light burning there as a warning to shipping of the hazards of the reef. This is the first record of a lighthouse in the Channel Islands.

The ruins of the priory chapel and the living quarters were investigated in September 1928 by Messrs A.D.B. Godfray, C. Langton, E.P. Le Sauvage, A.E. Mourant and N.V.L. Rybot. Their investigations revealed that the chapel was 10 feet 3 inches broad and 16 feet 6 inches long, with three windows, two in the east wall and one near the eastern end of the south wall. Between this last window and the east wall was a piscina. There was a door at the west end opening into the living quarters, which were in prolongation of the chapel and were 25 feet 8 inches long and 10 feet 3 inches broad.

The ruins of the chapel are illustrated in *The Ecréhous* by P.J. Ouless, published in Jersey in 1884.

ST OUEN'S MANOR CHAPEL is located in the grounds of St Ouen's Manor, St Ouen, Jersey. It is dedicated to St Anne, and is constructed of granite, roofed with tiles and has a belfry (with bell) at the apex of the west gable. There is an entrance in the west front and two in the north wall, one at the east end and the other at the west end. It has three narrow windows, one in the north wall and two in the south wall, and two larger ones, one in the east wall and one in the west front. The altar stone, with five consecration crosses, was probably originally in the Chapel of St George, which served the manors of Vinchelez de Haut and Vinchelez de Bas and no longer exists. There is a niche, about ground level, at the east end of the south wall. The chapel has a font consisting of a granite bowl mounted on a pillar. Around the outside of the bowl is an elaborate design consisting of a heart (the outlet hole) between two hands with sleeves and cuffs, one belonging to a man and the other to a woman. On the man's sleeve are the de Carteret arms with a label of four points: on the woman's sleeve is a flower with eight petals. The stained-glass windows are by H.T. Bosdet and depict the story of St Anne.

SAMARES MANOR CHAPEL, of which only the crypt survives, is incorporated in the west wing of Samarès Manor, Inner Road, St Clement, Jersey. The chapel, which it is believed was dedicated to St Martha, was built north and south and not east and west as was customary, causing some to doubt its ecclesiastical origins. The roof of the crypt is supported by two ancient pillars (the base of the north pillar was probably the capital of the south pillar) and there are moulded windows in the west wall.

ST APOLLINE'S CHAPEL (Our Lady of Perelle), La Grande Rue, St Saviour's, Guernsey, is the only existing building in the British Isles dedicated to St Apolline, the patron saint of dentists.

In 1392 Nicolas Henry obtained the consent of the abbot and monks of Mont St Michel, the Lords of the Manor, to found the chapel subject to his obtaining the permission of King Richard II of England. The King's permission was forthcoming in 1394 and no doubt the chapel was built shortly afterwards.

The building is stone-vaulted and roofed with old Cotswold

stone tiles. The western gable is surmounted by a belfry. The building has three square-headed windows, one in the east gable, one in the north wall and one in the south wall at the east end. It also has two round-headed doors, one in the west end of the north wall and one in the west end of the south wall.

The interior of the chapel is paved with York stone and the walls are plastered, At the end of the south wall to the right of where the altar once stood is a piscina. A simple altar of Purbeck stone was installed during the restoration (1978).

On the south wall is painted the *Last Supper*, said to be unusual because it depicts St Peter holding a sword over his shoulder and because the 'cups' are depicted as glass goblets with the wine showing through the bowls. Some of the figures have been lost through the ravages of time. It is believed that at one time all the walls were covered with frescoes.

The chapel has two stained-glass windows, one depicting Our Lady and the other the Long Melford Lily design.

LIHOU PRIORY CHURCH (St Mary of Lihou) stands on Lihou island off the west coast of Guernsey from which it is reached by a causeway when the tide allows. The priory is mentioned in a bull of Adrian IV, the only English Pope, dated 1155, where it is listed among the possessions of the Abbey of Mont St Michel. The priors were appointed by the monastery of St Michael of the Vale.

Only the ruins remain of the priory church, which in its final form had a nave with a stone-vaulted roof, a tower on the north side of the nave and a choir, which has been described as having been by local standards "a very elaborate structure of the twelfth century". A model of the chapel as it may have looked is on display in the Guernsey Museum.

The sanctuary was raised two feet above the level of the floor of the nave.

The church was paved with alternate glazed tiles of green and buff malachite 6½ inches square, some bearing designs, probably made in the Saintonge area of south-west France, and dating from the fifteenth century. A number of these tiles have been removed from the site owing to their brittle state, recorded on a large plan and stored in the hope that they will be displayed in a museum at some future time; the remainder are *in situ* covered with a sheet of polythene and a layer of soil and rubble to protect them.

A sculptured stone, formerly let into the wall of a house at Les Adams, St Peter's, showing a rough delineation of a church, said to be the priory church, a cross, the letters "HDM" and "LHM" and the date 1114 in Roman numerals, is preserved on the island.

Adjacent to the ruins of the church are those of the priory's domestic buildings.

Two graves have been found within the church, one in the chancel and one in the nave; other graves have been found outside the church, on the seaward side.

For centuries fishermen dipped the sails of their boats in honour of the priory of Our Lady of Lihou. In contrast, the coven of witches meeting at Le Catioroc or on the beach at Rocquaine shook their fists at the priory and screamed "Fall, fall from there! Mary of Lihou."

The parish of St Peter-in-the-Wood includes Lihou and in the past it has been known for a new rector to pay an extra fee on his induction for the plural benefice!

ST TUGUAL'S CHAPEL, Herm, stands close by the Manor House. Its patron saint was a Welsh monk who crossed over to Brittany and became Bishop of Tréguier. A charter of King Henry II of England dated some time between 1155 and 1158 gave the Island of Herm to the canons who were serving God there for the foundation in the island of a monastery for canons regular (No. 252 of the *Cartulaire*).

The chapel is built of granite, is stone-vaulted and has a separate little belfry. It is only 30 feet long and comprises a nave with a north transept. The window in the south wall, near the altar, is filled with stained glass depicting Christ in a boat stilling the water of the Sea of Galilee. The building is fully furnished and used for services.

Outside the chapel, adjacent to the entrance, is a pump dated 1867.

4

The Later Churches and Chapels of Jersey

ST AUBIN'S CHURCH (1889–92) stands on the east side of St Aubin's Hill, St Brelade. To-day it is known as St Aubin-on-the-Hill. It replaced an earlier church with the same dedication which stood on the site of what is now a car park, immediately to the north of the present church, although the ground was lowered when the car park was made. The church was intended to serve the population of St Aubin who found the journey to the parish church at the far end of St Brelade's Bay somewhat irksome. The foundation stone was laid in 1735 but the first service was not held until 1749. The building was declared unsafe in 1887. The present church is built of pink granite with lighter coloured granite dressings. The interior comprises a nave with two sides, a chancel with a chapel on its north side and a recess on its south side which houses the organ. The nave has slender granite pillars and a clerestory. The chancel is at a notably higher level than the nave and has a sedilia on its south side. The marble font stands at the west end of the nave. A number of the windows, including the large ones at the east and west ends, contain stained glass. Two are particularly worth noting. The first is by Edward Burne-Jones and William Morris (1894) and depicts two angels against a leafy background with below "The Annunciation" and "The Nativity"; the second by Bosdet depicts "The Marriage at Cana". The church owns a considerable collection of plate, including: two cups (1749), chalice (1914), flagon (1877), paten on foot (1846), paten (1888), platter (1749), baptismal dish and two collecting mugs, probably by Jean Gruchy, a Jersey silversmith, and one electroplated collecting mug. The church has a belfry at the east end of the roof containing one bell cast by Jean Bazin at Nantes in 1786.

Across the road from the church is a public pump standing in a recess, with a granite lintel, on which is carved the word "HARBOUR" and the date 1862.

It was not until after the ending of the Napoleonic Wars in 1815 when there was a vast increase in the population resulting largely from the settlement in the island of many retired naval and army officers and their families – the start of the British residents – that another Anglican Church, St James's, was built. In the years to follow it was to be joined by many more district churches and chapels-of-ease.

ST JAMES'S CHURCH (1827–29 – by Wigg & Co), St James's Street, St Helier, was at one time the garrison church. It is built of granite in a Gothic Revival style and has twin west towers with prickly pinnacles whose tops were amputated as they had become unsafe. The parapets of the walls are battlemented. The nave has a racked gallery. There is a window by Bosdet in the sanctuary; there is also a window (1962) depicting St James the Great and St Nicholas. The churchyard on the St James's Street side is bounded by iron railings and gates. The vicarage (1895) of pink granite stands adjacent to the church.

ALL SAINTS CHURCH (1834–35 – by James T. Parkinson), Parade, St Helier, was built on the site of the Strangers' Cemetery (1796). It is a plain building in the classical style. In the centre of the pediment is a clock. Resting against the exterior of the north wall of the building is a large granite stone to the memory of Anne Elie (née Guérinot) and Fanny Elie drowned in a wreck off Elizabeth Castle in 1825. Towards the base of the stone are carved the skull and crossbones.

ST MATTHEW'S CHURCH (1840–42 – by James T. Parkinson: reconstructed 1934 by A.B. Grayson), Millbrook, St Lawrence, is often referred to as 'The Glass Church' because of the considerable amount of Lalique glass which it contains. Although originally built as a chapel-of-ease it has now a parish of its own. In 1934 it was reconstructed as a memorial to the first Baron Trent of Nottingham, the founder of Boots the Chemists. Both the exterior and interior of the building are extremely plain. However, the interior is made beautiful by the lavish use of glass by René Lalique of Paris. The building comprises a vestibule, vestry, nave with a glass-fronted gallery and chancel with a Lady Chapel on one side and a vestry (now only used at weddings for the signing of the register) on the other. The windows and ceiling light-troughs are of glass. The altar and the large cross rising behind it with a matching pillar on either side are also glass (with a lily design), as are the communion rail between the nave and the chancel and the screens dividing the Lady Chapel and the vestry from the chancel and the nave. The striking group of four angels behind the altar in the Lady Chapel are of the same material. Another two glass angels are in the entrance doors. The font is almost certainly the only glass one in the British Isles and may be unique. The interior walls are faced with Bath stone, the floor of the chancel is paved with Dorset stone and that of the nave with Portland stone; the pulpit and lectern are made of Hopton Wood stone. The tower contains eight bells (by Gillett and Johnson) on which hymn tunes and music are played before the services.

Next to the church is the church hall built in 1954.

ST MARK'S CHURCH (1842–44 – by John Hayward), David Place, St Helier, is a pleasing Victorian church in the Gothic style, with a battlemented and pinnacled tower at its west end, surmounted by a hexagonal spire, topped by a weathercock – one of the landmarks of the town. In the west front of the tower is a clock (1880). The parapets of the north and south walls are also battlemented. Inside the building are a central porch and a south porch, decorated with murals, a nave, with a central aisle and two side aisles, and a gallery on each of its north, south and west sides, and a chancel. The roof is supported by slender wooden columns. The organ dating from 1872 was rebuilt in its centenary year. Many of the windows contain stained glass. The old reredos has been re-sited on the wall at the back of the west gallery. The church plate includes a silver gilt chalice (1844), another silver chalice and a silver gilt paten. The tower contains a ring of six bells of which the heaviest is the tenor weighing 9½ hundredweights. The churchyard on the David Place side is bounded by a fine set of railings and gates.

On the north side of the church stands the church hall and beyond is St Helier's rectory (1842 – by J.T. Parkinson), sometimes referred to as the 'Deanery', as more often than not the Rector of St Helier is also the Dean of Jersey.

GENERAL HOSPITAL CHAPEL (1846–48 – by John Hayward), Parade, St Helier, forms the centre-piece of a group of three Gothic Revival buildings on the north side of the hospital complex. It is built of granite and has a timber roof. In its north wall, above the altar, is a large window filled with stained glass (about 1895) in memory of John Bennett and his wife Elizabeth. The chapel contains a memorial (originally in the old chapel) to the memory of Charles Robin who left money in trust for an Anglican minister to be appointed to care for the spiritual health of the patients in the hospital. The chapel also has a polished granite font, a pair of eighteenth-century Canadian candlesticks, a beautifully carved pinewood Holy Ghost dove, which came from an old church in Beauce County, Quebec, and two kneelers embroidered with the parish emblems in front of the communion rail. A piece of crochet of "The Lord's Prayer" by Mrs A.M. Gallie is on the wall on the south side of the altar.

ST LUKE'S CHURCH (1848–51 – by John Hayward), Route du Fort, St Saviour, is built of granite with a slate roof and is cruciform in plan and consists of a nave, north and south transepts and a south porch. It has a belfry above the crossing. The nave has no aisles and the north transept is occupied by a chapel. There is a substantial font at the west end. The nave is divided from the chapel by a wrought-iron screen. The reredos has as its subject the "Last Supper". The church has lancet windows many of which are filled with stained glass, notably the triple lancet windows above the altar containing glass depicting "The Good Shepherd" by Bosdet. In the

LILLIE LANGTRY
1853 - 1929

Lille Langtry's memorial in the churchyard of St Saviour's Church, Jersey

St Anne's Church, Alderney

St Peter's Church, Sark

Gateway of Vale Castle, Vale, Guernsey

Fort Henry, Grouville, Jersey

Archirondel Tower,
St Martin, Jersey

Tower No. 6 L'Ancresse,
Vale, Guernsey: towers
Nos. 7 (*left*) and 9 (*right*)
appear in the distance

The old library, Library
Place, St Helier, Jersey

Almorah Crescent, St Helier,
Jersey

The music school at Victoria College, St Helier, Jersey

Constables' Office, St. Peter Port, Guernsey

The Golden Lion, Market Street, St Peter Port, Guernsey

Guernsey Museum and Art Gallery, Candie Gardens, St Peter Port – Museum of the Year, 1979

Les Mouriaux House, St Anne, Alderney

churchyard is the war memorial (1922). The splendid church hall (1949) stands adjacent to the east end of the church. It was a gift from T.B.F. Davis, a generous benefactor to his native island. Another of his benefactions is the very beautiful Howard Davis Park which borders St Luke's churchyard on its north and west sides. St Luke's vicarage stands opposite the church across the Route du Fort.

The most remarkable story concerning St Luke's relates to Davis. When he was a lad of fourteen he went to sea as a ship's boy in a Jersey-owned ship, the *Satellite*. The vessel ran aground on the Haisborough Sands off the coast of Norfolk. Davis answered the captain's appeal for a volunteer to man the punt in an endeavour to save the ship's papers and the captain's valuables, including his top hat. The painter broke and Davis was cast adrift. He sculled out to sea and managed to keep his small craft from being swamped by bailing it out with the hat. Thirty-six hours passed before Davis was picked up half-frozen by a small Norwegian vessel, but it was still to be some time before he was put ashore at Cowes in the Isle of Wight. He eventually got back to Jersey on the very day when he was being remembered in the Sunday morning service at St Luke's. He arrived after the service had started and sat in a pew at the back of the church. When it was over he presented himself to what must have been an astonished vicar, Canon Philip R.P. Braithwaite.

ST SIMON'S CHURCH (1865–66 – by George Frederick Bodley), Great Union Road, St Helier, is in the early Decorated style. The interior consists of a nave, south aisle and a chancel. The north aisle and campanile, although included in the architect's design, have never been completed. The building is principally constructed of granite but the interior arches and columns are of Caen stone. The oak altar-table was designed by the architect. The font, also designed by the architect, is circular and made of pinkish alabaster and rests on columns of polished Purbeck marble. Suspended above the west end of the chancel is a striking hanging rood. On the right of the altar is a carved stone recess, resembling a piscina, presented to the church by Charles George Renouf in 1866. It is made of Chausey granite and is said to date from between 1350 and 1450. It was brought from No. 14 Royal Square and it has been suggested that it was removed there from St Helier's parish church after the Reformation. However, this is unlikely. The church contains a number of stained-glass windows including one to Charles I, King and Martyr, and another to Archbishop William Laud.

ST PAUL'S CHURCH (1891 – by Adolphus Curry), New Street, St Helier, is a proprietary chapel. It stands on the site of another church with the same dedication built in 1815 and demolished in 1889. The building is in the Gothic style and constructed of pink granite with grey granite dressings and roofed with slates. There is an open belfry at the east end of the roof. Iron railings and gates divide the churchyard from the street.

ST ANDREW'S CHURCH (1926–27 – by C.W. Blanchard Bolton), First Tower, St Helier, is built of granite and stands on a site adjacent to First Tower Park. It has a tower with octagonal corner turrets at its west end. The tower contains a carillon of bells and has a clock on its south side. The pillars of the nave are of granite as is the substantial pulpit (1948). A number of the windows contain stained glass including the three-light east window and the similar west window. Altogether it is a very attractive twentieth-century church.

Adjacent to the building stands the brick-built community centre (1978).

GOURAY (ST MARTIN'S) CHURCH (1832–33: partially rebuilt and extended 1915), Gorey Hill, St Martin, stands in a commanding position above Gorey Village. It is a simple building having a square tower with a battlemented parapet, surmounted by a low octagonal spire bearing a weathercock. The tower has a clock and contains one bell cast by John Warner & Sons Ltd in London in 1895.

ST PETER'S CHURCH (1851), La Rocque, Grouville, is a small granite-built structure consisting of a nave with lancet windows, a south porch and a bell turret. The east window contains stained glass.

ST GEORGE'S CHURCH (1876–80 – by Hayward & Son), La Rue du Nord, St Ouen, is built of granite and has a saddleback tower. Inside it comprises a nave and chancel.

ANGLICAN/METHODIST COMMUNICARE CENTRE (1976 – by Messrs Nigel Biggar & Partners), is situated at Les Quennevais, St Brelade. The foundation stone was laid by Queen Elizabeth the Queen Mother. The main hall is known as the Markland Hall in memory of Thomas Markland who was a major benefactor of the building project. The building incorporates the foundation stone from Tabor Methodist Chapel, demolished some years ago. A window to the memory of Laurence Hargreaves, a founder member of the centre's funding trust, was presented by his widow in 1979. It was designed by Lawrence Lee and has for its theme the hymn "Lord of All Being Throned Afar" and depicts "The Creation" in the upper panel and a symbolic design in the lower.

Methodism was introduced into Jersey in 1774 and gained ground rapidly resulting in the building of a large number of churches either in the Neo-classical or Gothic Revival styles of architecture. Some of the churches such as St Ouen, Sion and Royal Crescent (now demolished) are very large and resemble classical temples; others are small and very simple in design. To-day eighteen churches remain in use as places of worship, as follows: Wesley-Grove (formerly Grove Place) (1846–47 – by Philip Brée: restoration 1901 – by Adolphus Curry) forming a terminal to the north end of Halkett Place, St Helier, is in the classical style with a tastefully decorated interior; Aquila Road (1839), St Helier, is also in the classical style and contains a lectern installed in memory of Cecil Stanley Harrison, C.M.G., O.B.E., Bailiff of Jersey (1961–62), a life-long member of the church; Bethesda (1868), St Peter; Bethlehem (1829), St Mary; Ebenezer (1881), Trinity; Eden (1833), St Saviour; First Tower (1847) in the district of that name; Galaad (1832), St Lawrence; Georgetown-Royal Crescent (formerly Georgetown) (1872–73 – by Messrs Le

Sueur & Brée), Georgetown, St Saviour, is in the classical style with fine granite pillars inside, and a good modern hall standing alongside; Gorey (1840), Gorey Village, Grouville; La Rocque (1897), Grouville, in the Gothic Revival style; Philadelphie (formerly St Peter's) (1825: enlarged 1835); St Aubin (1868), The Bulwarks, St Aubin, is a pleasant granite-built church in the Gothic Revival style, with the old chapel (1817), now used as a hall, at the rear; St Martin (1851) in the parish of the same name; St Ouen (1869–71 – by Philip Brée) in the parish of the same name, is no longer used for services which are now held in the original St Ouen's Chapel (1809), the oldest Methodist church in the island; Samarès (1903), Coast Road, St Clement; Sion (1881), St John; Six Roads (Six Rues) (1859–61), St Lawrence, is a fine granite-built church in the Gothic Revival style. Other chapels survive but are no longer used for worship. These include Wesley (1876), Wesley Street, Great Union Road (1825) and Seaton Place (1868), all in St Helier; Augrès (1833), Trinity, now a private art gallery with fourteen granite plaques let into the exterior of the south wall each bearing the initials of a member of the congregation who gave £5 towards the building of a Sunday school, and Les Frères (1912), St John, now used for youth activities.

As a direct result of the influx of French royalist refugees, Roman Catholicism returned to Jersey. Five oratories were established on the island: de St Malo (ceased 1801), St Louis or du Port (ceased 1801), des Sts Anges (ceased 1803), du Sacré Coeur (ceased 1801), and St Pierre at St Aubin, with possibly another at Gorey. These oratories served the refugees and it was not until 1803 that a permanent chapel, dedicated to St Louis, was opened in Castle Street, St Helier. It was closed in 1842 and replaced by St Thomas's, New Street, St Helier, the predecessor of the present church of that name. By the time the Napoleonic Wars had ended in 1815 the royalist refugees had melted away. However, what the newly re-established Roman Catholic Church in Jersey lost by their disappearance was made up for by the French who settled in Jersey when peace came and by the arrival in the island of appreciable numbers of Irish immigrants, practically all of whom were Roman Catholics.

ST MARTIN'S (R.C.) CHURCH (1862–63), St Martin's Main Road, St Martin, was founded as a result of the large number of Irish and French living in the parish. The building is of granite and is in the Gothic style. Behind the church is the tombstone of Colonel Charles Edward Stuart (died 1880) who believed himself to be the great-grandson of the Young Pretender and the rightful King of England.

ST MARY'S AND ST PETER'S CHURCH (1865–67 – by Joseph Hansom, inventor of the Hansom Cab: extension 1891) stands in Vauxhall Street, St Helier. The previous church (1841–43 – by James T. Parkinson) which formed the west end of Hansom's church, was demolished in 1965 and replaced by a new frontage, since partly removed. The present building is in Early English style. The pillars are composed of single blocks of Jersey granite. The timber hammer-beam roof is extremely lofty. Immediately to the west of the church stands the granite-built school house (1862).

ST MATTHIEU'S CHURCH (1871–72 – by Alfred Frangeul), Coin Varin, St Peter, was named in honour of Matthieu de Gruchy (1761–97), a Jerseyman, who while prisoner in France had turned Roman Catholic and became a priest. He died tragically in Nantes before a firing squad on 28 November 1797. The church is in the Gothic style and comprises a nave, tribune, transepts and apse.

ST THOMAS'S CHURCH (1883–87 – by Alfred Frangeul), Val Plaisant, St Helier, is built in the Gothic style and is undoubtedly the finest Roman Catholic church in Jersey. It is constructed of pink granite from La Moye and grey granite from Brittany and roofed with tiles. It has a tower surmounted by a spire topped by a cross, one of the landmarks of the town. The top of the cross is 196 feet above the ground. There is a clock in the front face of the tower. The interior of the building comprises a nave with clerestory, aisles, crossing, transepts, chancel and a number of chapels. The gallery over the porch, projecting into the nave, houses the organ (1959 – by Henry Willis and Sons). Many of the windows are of stained glass. Behind the pulpit there is a monument to the Reverend Father Michaux, the founder of the church. On either side there are two small slabs on which are recorded the names of the bishops and priests since 1792. The belfry contains five bells.

ST JOSEPH'S CHURCH (1893: enlarged 1902 and 1909) at the corner of La Rue au Blancq and Grouville Road, Grouville, is a plain building with some stained-glass windows, the high altar from Maison St Louis, a pipe organ from Beaulieu Convent and a bell presented in 1954.

ST JOHN AND ST ANTHONY (1924), Ville-à-l'Evêque, Trinity, is a small granite-built church with a belfry above its porch (1974 – by J.H. Richards).

SACRED HEART (1936–47 – by Julien Barbier), Victoria Road, St Aubin, is a beautiful granite-built church. The representation of an anchor built into the granite above the main door was put there by the mason concerned to commemorate the sinking of the *Graf Spee* in 1939.

ST PATRICK'S CHURCH (1948–49), Inner Road, St Clement, is a simple modern building with a light and airy interior comprising a nave, transepts, chancel, baptistry and sacristy. It has a fine granite altar and altar rails and a granite font. It also possesses three stained-glass windows. The one over the principal entrance depicting the Magi presenting their gifts was bequeathed by Frederick William Knight (died 1950), a parishioner and a benefactor of the church; the one in the chancel is a window shaped like a cross and depicts the Holy Eucharist; the one in the baptistry depicts an anchor and was given in memory of George Louis Boudin (died 1975).

During the nineteenth century and the present century a large number of churches belonging to other denominations have been built some of which are of architectural interest.

ST JOHN'S UNITED REFORMED CHURCH (formerly
Congregational) (1809–10), St John's Main Road, St John,
was built of Jersey materials, the local farmers carting the
granite. Originally it had a thatched roof which was replaced
in the 1820s.

THE EVANGELICAL FREE CHAPEL (1819), Maufant, St
Saviour, a plain building with a small entrance porch, still
exists, although no longer used as a place of worship.

NEW CHURCH (formerly New Jerusalem Temple) (1848),
Victoria Street, St Helier, is also a plain building bearing the
date on its frontage.

BAPTIST CHURCH (1851), Vauxhall Street, St Helier, is in
the Neo-classical style.

EVANGELICAL CHURCH (1854–55 – by Messrs Poulton &
Woodman), Halkett Place, St Helier, replaced a previous
church built in 1808. It is in the Gothic style and built of grey
granite with dressings, originally of Caen stone. The interior
of the building is in the shape of a lengthened octagon with
tall Caen stone columns and a central roof-lantern. Iron railings and gates divide the churchyard from the road. Behind
the church and fronting on Cattle Street is the Evangelical
Church Hall (Lyric Hall) (1860) now used for services but
originally used only for the Sunday-school.

ST COLUMBA'S CHURCH OF SCOTLAND (in the past often
called the 'Scotch Church') (1857–59 – by James Hine),
Midvale Road, St Helier, is in the Gothic style and built of
dark grey granite, with re-constituted stone dressings (originally of Caen stone) and roofed with slates. It has a tower surmounted by a spire at its north-east corner. It has a nave with
east and west transepts and a gallery at the rear. The east transept houses the organ. The carved pew ends are in the form of
fleurs-de-lis. In the north gable is a large six-light window
with a series of small windows beneath. To the west of the
church stands the church hall (1874) built of pink granite.

UNITED REFORMED CHURCH (formerly Congregational) (1860–61 – by Philip Brée), Victoria Street, St Helier, is in the Gothic style and built of granite. The spire was demolished in 1968.

5

The Later Churches and Chapels of Guernsey, Alderney and Sark

TRINITY CHURCH (1789), Trinity Square, St Peter Port, is in the classical style with Dutch gables. The walls are stuccoed and the dressings and the quoins are of granite. In the apex of the main frontage is a clock and above is an open granite belfry (1887) containing a chime of three bells. The interior of the building comprises a vestibule, nave and gallery. Above both of the doors giving access from the vestibule to the nave is a round stained-glass window. The one above the south door depicts the arms of Guernsey; that above the north door depicts the sign of the Trinity. The church has box pews, a pulpit carved with the story of the prodigal son and a marble font, both from St James-the-Less, a second font and a brass lectern. In the sanctuary are two panels on which are set out the Ten Commandments. All the exterior windows are of plain glass except for that in the baptistry which came from St Barnabas's Church and was inserted in 1930, and a cross in the fanlight above the main entrance. The church plate includes: two chalices, a flagon and a paten on foot, all bearing the London hallmark for 1820, two chalices and a paten on foot all bearing the London hallmark for 1840, and an alms-dish and spoon bearing the London hallmark for 1897.

ST JAMES-THE-LESS CHURCH (1818 – by John Wilson) stands in the apex formed by College Street and St James Street where they converge to join Grange Road, St Peter Port. It has now ceased to be a church and is a protected building in the ownership of the States. The church, in the Neo-classical style, is built of stone, with dressed stone facings to the windows, and roofed with slates. It has a portico of six columns supporting a pediment with a clock at its centre. Rising from the west end of the church is a tower with a circular belfry above which is a gallery surmounted by a dome topped by a weathervane. The interior of the building comprises a circular vestibule, nave, with horseshoe-shaped gallery supported on slender Doric columns, apse and vestry. In the belfry is a bell dated 1823 cast by Mears.

ST JOHN'S CHURCH (1836–38 – by Robert Payne), Les Amballes, St Peter Port, is granite-built and roofed with slates. It has a tower with angle buttresses at its east end. Above the front entrance is a stone bearing the date 1836 and above that in the east face of the tower is a clock. The church plate includes: two identical chalices and two identical patens bearing the London hallmark for 1836, presented by Lady de Saumarez, the widow of Admiral Lord de Saumarez, who on 16 June 1836 laid the foundation stone of the church, his last public act; two identical chalices bearing the Chester hallmark for 1901; a flagon bearing the London hallmark for 1836, also presented by Lady de Saumarez; an alms-dish, probably electroplated. The church has a ring of three bells cast by John Warner & Sons in 1887 and installed to commemorate the Diamond Jubilee of Queen Victoria. In the churchyard stands the war memorial.

ST JOSEPH'S AND ST MARY'S (1846–51 – by Augustus Welby Pugin: spire 1885 – by P.P. & S.P. Pugin), Cordier Hill, St Peter Port, stands in a commanding position above the town and its copper broach spire rising to a height of 150 feet is a notable landmark. The church is built of dark-coloured granite with white stone dressings. The interior consists of a nave with two aisles and a chancel with a chapel on either side. A number of the windows contain stained glass, and the stations of the cross are of wood. In the north entrance porch under the tower at the north-west corner of the building are two marble tablets, one recording the opening of the church by Cardinal Wiseman in 1851, and the other its consecration by Bishop Virtue in 1885. The tower contains a chime of eleven bells, all cast at the Whitechapel foundry. The earliest bell is dated 1851 and the latest 1951.

ST MATTHEW'S (1852–54 – by J. Johnson of London), Cobo, Castel, is built of red granite in the Norman style with an apsidal chancel and a central open bell-turret with two small bells. The stonework is excellent. In the church is a chair (1963) to the memory of Marianne Miller (née Carey) who conceived the idea of building St Matthew's. The church plate includes: a chalice bearing the London hallmark for 1855, a chalice bearing the London hallmark for 1851, a paten on foot bearing the London hallmark for 1846, a platter bearing the London hallmark for 1843, and a flagon bearing the London hallmark for 1849. The bell-turret, bells and lych-gate were given by the Reverend William Thomas Collings when the church was built.

ST STEPHEN'S CHURCH (1862–65 – by George Frederick Bodley), Les Gravées, St Peter Port, is built of grey and red granite laid in courses. The interior, which is rather dark, consists of a nave, with a clerestory composed of circular windows, a north and south aisle, and a chancel with a chapel on either side. The nave is divided from its aisles by Caen stone arches with differing capitals to the pillars. At its east end are four fine red granite columns, two on either side; at its west end is an organ loft added in 1930. The west window is filled with a splendid stained-glass "Tree of Jesse" by William Morris's firm, far the best window in the building. The church plate includes: a plain silver-gilt chalice bearing the London hallmark for 1904, a silver-gilt chalice, chased and set with precious stones, bearing the London hallmark for 1898, a paten bearing the London hallmark for 1899, and two cha-lices, two patens and a flagon bearing the London hallmark for 1864. The church has one bell which hangs in an aperture in the gable over the north porch.

ST BARNABAS'S CHURCH (1872–74 – by Sir Arthur Blomfield), Tower Hill, St Peter Port, was built as a memo-rial to the Reverend Charles Guille. It is a large building in the Gothic style with a tower with a pyramidical spire on its north side. It is built of Cobo granite, blue granite and red brick and roofed with red tiles. Having become redundant the church was closed and purchased by the States to house the Island and Lukis Museum, which in turn was closed as the building had become unsafe. St Barnabas's is one of a number of landmarks which make up St Peter Port's distinctive skyline.

ST ANDREW'S CHURCH (1897 – by William Murray), The Grange, St Peter Port, is built of dark grey granite. It has a bell tower to the right of the front entrance and a small spire above the main roof and a porch at the main entrance. On the front of the tower is a sundial.

LES VAUXBELETS CHAPEL (1923–25 – by Brother Déodat), St Andrew's, is one of the best-known sights of Guernsey. It is a diminutive building with a steeple surmounted by a cross, crypts and a grotto. It is built of concrete encrusted with a kind of mosaic made up of pebbles, ormer shells and countless pieces of china. The result is far more pleasing to the eye than could be imagined from the description. The interior of the chapel has a nave and a chancel, at a slightly higher level, with four small windows. Above the altar is a small figure of the Virgin Mary and nearby, are the steps leading to the crypts.

OUR LADY OF THE ROSARY (1961–62 – by A. Seguin), Burnt Lane, St Peter Port, is a very beautiful church. The present building replaces one dedicated to St Mary and dating from 1829 which was the only Roman Catholic church in Guernsey until 1851 when the opening of St Joseph's and St Mary's Church caused its closure. The old church was re-opened in 1861 and remained in use until its replacement by the new building. The design of the present church is based on two themes, the ship and the mysteries of the rosary. The roof is in the shape of an upturned hull, as was that of the old church, and behind the altar is a mast to which the triptych, *Annunciation, Crucifixion* and *Visitation* by P. Lejeune, is joined like a sail. On either side of the mast are halyards on which hang the flags of England, France, the Virgin Mary and the Pope. The altar is of Finnish granite, weighs one and a half tons and contains the relics of five saints, including St Sampson and St Maglorius. The stations of the cross comprise a series of pen and ink drawings by P. Lejeune, who also designed the three stained-glass windows depicting the Nativity, Pentecost and the Rosary. The font is of Finnish granite with a bronze cover. The church possesses four beautiful statues by J. Cattant – the Virgin Mary with Jesus standing on Her knees (in bronze near the altar) and St Louis of France, St Anne of Brittany and St Thérèse of Lisieux (in oak near the entrance). At the front of the building are two panels giving its history, and beside it is a belfry built in 1979 to commemorate its 150th anniversary.

EBENEZER METHODIST CHURCH (1815; renovated 1886 and 1960), Brock Road, St Peter Port, is built of grey granite in the Gothic Revival style. It has a tower with angle buttresses and an octagonal spire. The large interior comprises a nave, transepts and chancel.

MORLEY CHAPEL (1863), Fort Road, St Peter Port, is no longer used as a place of worship. It is a fine building in the Gothic Revival style and constructed of red granite. It consists of a nave, transepts and chancel with lancet windows. The three-light stained-glass window depicting "Christ the Good Shepherd" was removed to Rohais Methodist Church in 1959 having been re-set in clear glass with new roundels by Miss M.E. de Putron. At the back of the chapel is the schoolroom, also no longer used for its original purpose.

Two early non-conformist churches worth noting are the Evangelical Congregational Church, La Villiaze, St Andrew's (1815), and the United Reformed Church, Grande Rue, St Saviour's (1817).

ST ANNE'S CHURCH (1847–50 – by Sir George Gilbert Scott), St Anne, Alderney, was built at the cost of the Reverend Canon John Le Mesurier, son of Lieutenant-General John Le Mesurier (1781–1843), the last hereditary Governor of Alderney, and Martha Le Mesurier (née

Perchard), his wife, in memory of his parents.

The story of how the church came to be built is rather charmingly told by Mrs Louisa Lane Clarke in her book *The Island of Alderney* (1851) as follows:

> Now it happened that the last Governor of the island, although the eldest of a large family to whom he was a kind and noble brother, was himself long childless – thirteen years childless; when, to the unspeakable joy of himself and his dear wife, God gave them the blessing of two living sons. As soon as the first was born – even in the first month – the grateful mother founded the Mouriaux School, and with her own hand wrote out the rules and lessons still used there; and when the second son was born, he was dedicated by his parents to the service of God, in a hope that was not disappointed. Years passed away, – the youngest son became the only one, – and he had scarcely fulfilled the desire of his parents by entering into the ministry of Christ's Church, when they died, the one three years before the other, leaving only this other wish for their child to realize.

A NEW PARISH CHURCH FOR ALDERNEY

There it stands, a free gift to the beloved island, and the offering of filial love, – a meet temple for Christian worship.

During the Occupation the church was used by the Germans as a general store and most of the pews and the six bells were removed. Damage was also caused to the fabric. After the war the building underwent a restoration which was completed by the end of 1953.

St Anne's is in the transitional style from Norman to Early English and is built of Alderney stone with quoins and finishings of Caen stone. It has a square central tower with a pyramidal spire. The building has a spacious interior comprising a nave, north and south aisles, transepts, chancel, terminating in an apse, and Lady Chapel.

The font is of Caen stone and stands near the south door. The stone on which the priest stands during a baptism was taken from the font of old St Anne's Church.

On the west wall are six brass plates, including the dedication plate, three to the north of the door and three to the south, outlining the history of the Le Mesurier family from 1684 to 1803. The six plaques commemorate respectively from south to north Thomas Le Mesurier, John Le Mesurier, Peter Le Mesurier, Henry Le Mesurier, John Le Mesurier and Peter Le Mesurier.

In the north transept is the Memorial Chapel containing five flags and the Roll of Honour. The Creed and the Lord's Prayer both in English and French are painted on the walls of the apse. The bishop's chair was given by Mrs Le Brun in memory of her husband who was vicar from 1886 to 1929. The screen at the west end of the Lady Chapel was carved by members of the Batiste family.

Many of the windows are filled with stained glass. The modern window above the west door depicts children of all races. A window on the north side commemorates Vincent William Ryan, the first Bishop of Mauritius, who was vicar from 1834 to 1846. The Victorian window above the high altar was restored in 1953. A window in the Lady Chapel commemorates the visit of Queen Elizabeth II to the island in 1957.

The church has six bells recast by Messrs John Taylor and Company in 1953 out of the metal of the original bells of which two were found in Alderney and four outside Cherbourg. The bells are all inscribed "C. AND G. MEARS, LONDON 1849" and "RECAST 1953" and bear the Loughborough foundry mark; in addition they bear the following inscriptions: the treble "ALL THINGS ARE READY" – in memory of B.B., H.B. and R. Bickerton; the second "PRAISE YE THE LORD"; the third "IN EVERYTHING GIVE THANKS"; the fourth "PRAISE YE THE LORD"; the fifth "O COME, LET US WORSHIP" – F.L. Impey; and the tenor "THE TIME IS SHORT, WATCH AND PRAY ALWAYS – DAISE MIGNOT – THIS RING OF SIX BELLS WAS RESTORED TO COMMEMORATE THE CORONATION OF QUEEN ELIZABETH II IN THE YEAR 1953".

The parish registers start in 1662 and are complete except for burials 1723–31 and a few small gaps.

Over the south entrance porch is a sculpture of the Good Shepherd bearing a lamb and on either side of the entrance is a small carved head. There are similar heads on either side of the west entrance.

The gateway, with wrought-iron gates, giving access to the churchyard from Victoria Street was erected in 1864 to the memory of the Prince Consort.

ST PETER'S CHURCH (1820: chancel added 1880), Sark, is a plain granite building. It has a square tower (raised in height since it was first built), with a pyramidical roof surmounted by a weathercock, and a clock with a face on all four sides.

The interior of the building comprises a nave and a chancel. The pulpit was given in memory of the Reverend J.L.V. Cachemaille, a former minister of Sark and author of *The Island of Sark*; the brass lectern was given in memory of the Reverend Charles Vermeil, also a former minister; the credence table was given in memory of Dorothy La Trobe-Bateman.

A number of stained-glass windows by Moore and Son, London, were installed in 1926. The first was given by Thomas de Carteret, the second was given in memory of the men of Sark who were killed in World War I, the third was given by Captain Marden in memory of his wife, the fourth was given by Major Ingram and his pupils and the fifth by the Misses Hale in memory of their family. There is a modern stained-glass window to St Maglorius, a memorial to members of the Hotton family. Another window depicts St John.

The church has a memorial to Helier de Carteret (1532–81), the first Lord of Sark, as well as memorials to Peter Le Pelley (died by drowning in 1839), Lord of Sark, and John William Falle and William Slowley Falle (died by drowning in 1903).

The church owns a chalice bearing the London hallmark possibly for 1675, a silver-gilt chalice and paten on foot bearing the London hallmark for 1732, another chalice bearing the mark of Guillaume Henry, a Guernsey silversmith, presented in 1765, a spoon and an electroplated flagon.

The bell is dated 1883 and was made at the cost of several friends out of two six-pounder field guns formerly used by the Sark Militia by A. Havard of Villedieu. It bears the names of William Frederick Collings, Lord of Sark, and C. Vermeil, the Minister.

6

The Fortifications of Jersey

MONT ORGUEIL CASTLE, otherwise known as Gorey Castle, one of the best known and most photographed sights in the island, stands on an elevated site above Gorey Harbour, St Martin. The date of its foundation is not known, but it was probably built shortly after 1204, although it is first mentioned in 1212. The castle was once a formidable fortification and virtually impregnable, but with the coming of cannon into general use this impregnability ceased as the building could be dominated by cannon planted on St Nicholas Mount which faces it on the landward side.

The castle would have been allowed to fall into decay had it not been for Sir Walter Ralegh (Governor 1600–03) who had a regard for the old place and wrote "it is a stately fort of great capacity, both as to maintenance and comfort . . . it were a pity to cast it down. . . ." In the event it was retained, although over the years it fell largely into ruins. It saw service during the English Civil War and again during the Napoleonic Wars, when it was the headquarters of the Jersey Naval Station commanded by Philip d'Auvergne, Duke of Bouillon, and yet again during the Occupation when the Germans made it into a self-contained strong point.

The castle consists of an outer ward, a lower ward, a middle ward, the old keep, the newer keep and the north-east outworks. The entrance from the castle green is by way of a road which passes through the first gate to the right of and attached to the Harliston Tower dating from the 1470s and to the left of the west barbican before reaching the outer ward at the second gate to which is attached the porter's lodge. The south side of the outer ward is bounded by the Parade Battery with a tower at either end. Beyond the south-west tower is the Water

Battery (1802). The east side is bounded by a wall pierced by a sally port and machicolated at its north end. On the north side, set into the wall of de Carteret's Rampart, are the arms of King Charles II (1660).

At the north-east corner of the lower ward is a stone staircase which gives access to the middle ward. It passes through the third or Queen's Gate where there is a stone slab let into the arch commemorating the visit of Queen Victoria and Prince Albert to the castle on 3 September 1846. It then continues through the fourth or Queen Elizabeth's Gate, which bears the Queen's Arms with the date 1593, the Poulett Family Arms and Anthony Poulett's Arms with the initials "APL" and "KN", the latter being those of Poulett's wife, Katherine Norreys. Beyond the gate is Peyton's Bulwark and the guard rooms with the middle ward beyond.

On the north side of the middle ward is a square building (now in ruins) known by the name of St George's Hall. Behind this building rises the massive bulk of the Somerset Tower, a solid structure built to support a gun platform, with shields carved with the cross of St George at intervals around its crenellated parapet. The platform is paved with flagstones and is reached by a flight of steps from the roof of the newer keep. On the east side of the middle ward are the remains of St George's Chapel with a crypt beneath (*see* Chapter III). Beyond the chapel are the Busgros Tower, once a prison, and the Cornish Bastion, bearing the arms of Henry Cornish dated 1547.

Continuing up into the castle from the middle ward with the Somerset Tower on the right, the entrance to the belltower is passed on the left and shortly afterwards, on the same side (as the steps bear to the right), the well house covering the well, which is 57 feet deep. On the left at the top of the steps, opposite the Mount Gate, access may be obtained to the Grand Battery, which faces on one side St Nicholas Mount and on the other St Catherine's Bay. Approximately half way along the west wall is the belfry and at the south-west corner is a tower. At the north-east corner is the Rochefort Tower, the north-east outworks and a sally port with further outworks known as the New Braye beyond and at a lower level.

Above the fifth, King Edward VI's or Mount Gate is a stone bearing the date 1551. Within the gate is the Long Gallery. Immediately on the right (looking inwards) is the guardroom and beyond that on the same side is an open space originally containing two storeys; on the left is St Mary's Chapel and Crypt (*see* Chapter III). Beyond the chapel on the east side of the castle are the Corbelled Tower, the Watch Tower and the south-west or Prynne's Tower, where William Prynne was imprisoned 1637–40. Access may be had from the chapel into the newer keep which consists of four storeys. The three upper storeys contained living quarters and are connected by a spiral staircase; the lowest known as the Artillery Store is entered from St Mary's Crypt. In the living quarters are fireplaces, two in the top storey, which at one time may have been divided, are of Tudor design. The smaller fireplace has scratched on it the motto of the Poulett Family *Gardez la Foi* and "R Warwick", presumably for Robinson Rich, Earl of Warwick, who was Governor in 1643. All the rooms have windows facing westwards with a magnificent view across the Royal Bay of Grouville. The top of the castle is surmounted by German observation towers.

The museum occupies the top storey of the newer keep, and there is a series of *tableaux* in adjacent parts of the castle.

LES CATEAUX (otherwise called Le Chastel Sedement) is the name of an ancient earthwork situated in the parish of Trinity which consisted of outer defences and a rampart or keep. It has been suggested that this fortification originated and was in use between 1204 and 1452, but there is a possibility, albeit remote, that the earthwork is prehistoric and not medieval.

GROSNEZ CASTLE occupied the whole of the headland at the extreme north-west of the island in the parish of St Ouen. Little is known of its history other than that it was in ruins by 1540. The perimeter wall, probably incorporating five bastions, was approximately 250 yards long and enclosed an area roughly circular in shape containing a number of small buildings. Steep cliffs protected the site on three sides and the landward side had the strongest defences including a battlemented gatehouse with a portcullis. Across the neck of the headland was a ditch spanned by a drawbridge. To-day all that remains of the castle are the ruins of the gatehouse, the foundations of some of the small buildings within the walls and the ditch. Twelve corbels found when the ditch was excavated are now to be seen in the Archaeological Museum at La Hougue Bie. On six are carved human heads, on another is carved a hand and on the remainder are carved designs, mostly geometrical. One head bears a crown; another has its tongue out.

ST AUBIN'S FORT stands on an islet off the town of St Aubin. It was started in 1542 and underwent many changes during the three succeeding centuries until eventually assuming its present form. The main feature of the building is the tower, originally only one storey high, around which grew up outer defence works. In 1643 bulwarks were built around the tower, and between before 1680 and 1700 a pier was built at the north-east corner of the islet to be followed by a line of quays or wharves along the north side of the islet, started before 1742 and completed by 1800. Additions and alterations were made to the fort itself between 1737 and 1837 and further work was carried out at the fort in 1839. Finally, the Germans carried out further works during the Occupation. To-day the building serves as an outdoor activity centre for young people.

ELIZABETH CASTLE stands on an islet in line with West Park slipway, St Helier, and may be reached by a causeway when the tide is out and by boat or amphibious craft when the tide is in. The castle, named after Queen Elizabeth I, was begun 1550–51 and completed by Paul Ivy, the military engineer, between 1590 and 1601 and occupies the site of the Priory of St Helier. The building was in continuous use as a fortification from the time of its inception until early in the twentieth century, and was modified and added to as occasion demanded.

At the end of the causeway is the first gate with Fort Charles (1646–47) standing to the right and to the rear. There are three recesses over the gate intended for the royal arms and those of the Governor and Lieutenant-Governor of the day. Above the gate is the belfry containing the castle's bell. Within the gate is the guard-house re-fronted in 1755.

Once inside the castle the main path proceeds southwards with the north-east bastion and then the east bastion on the left to the second gate which bears the arms of King William III (1697), Lord Jermyn, Governor of Jersey (1684–1704) and Lieutenant-Colonel Collier, Lieutenant-Governor (1695–1715). Adjacent to the east bastion is a projecting circular sentry-box with a conical roof.

Having passed under the second gate the path continues southwards, with the west bastion immediately to the right, through the outer ward with the Grand Battery with its armament of carronades, also on the right, to the drawbridge (which can no longer be drawn back) above the ditch and the third gate with the main guard above it. At the western end of the Grand Battery is another circular sentry-box. To east and west, just before the third gate, is a sally port. The key-stone of the west sally port bears the cypher of King George II and the date 1734.

Within the third gate is the lower ward where are the cells and the canteen, officers' quarters (now a café), the gymnasium (1726) (now the Militia Museum), the magazine bearing the arms of Sir John Lanier, Governor of Jersey (1679–84), dated 1682, and the barracks. Standing in the centre of the barrack square is a granite cross (1959) marking the site of the abbey of St Helier founded 1155.

The upper ward is reached from the lower ward through the fourth or Iron Gate and the fifth or Queen Elizabeth's Gate, bearing the Queen's Arms, beneath a Tudor Rose, above the arch and the arms of Sir Anthony Poulett, Governor of Jersey (1590–1600), impaling those of Katherine Poulett (née Norreys), his wife, on the left shoulder. On the left immediately before reaching the fifth gate is Ralegh's Yard.

The upper ward contains the north end of the Captain's House, the Governor's House (in which *tableaux* are displayed), the magazine and at the very top the mount. The doorway of the Governor's House bears on the right side the arms of William Fortescue with the initials "WF" and on the left side the arms of John Wadham with the initials "JW". Cut into the rock beside the steps leading to the mount is a merchant's mark dated 1601.

The Germans occupied the castle during the Occupation and carried out work on the defences. There is an exhibition of German military equipment in the courtyard bunker.

A splendid view of St Helier's Hermitage (*see* Chapter III) and the breakwater may be had from the south side of the lower ward.

TOWERS. A series of thirty-one towers were built around the coasts of Jersey between 1779 and 1835. There were twenty-three in the first group built between 1779 and 1801, three in the second built between 1808 and about 1814, and five in the third built 1834–35.

General Conway, Governor of Jersey (1772–95), conceived the idea of building thirty towers for the defence of Jersey in 1778, sixteen years before the Royal Navy put out of action the round tower at Mortella Point in Corsica prior to capturing the island. Although most of the surviving Jersey towers are referred to, irrespective of design, as 'martello' towers, only those in the third group of towers, four of which survive, were of the English 'martello' design.

The towers in the first group, of which seventeen (which includes La Rocco, Archirondel and Seymour Towers) survive, are built of stone and the walls are pierced on two floors by loopholes. The dimensions of a Jersey tower are approximately as follows: height 36 feet; diameter at base 34 feet; walls 8 feet thick at the base decreasing to 6 feet at the top. Projecting from the parapet around the flat roof are four machicolated galleries for observation and for firing downwards on an enemy.

The towers in the second group differ in design from those in the first and third group. In shape they resemble an upturned flower pot without a rim.

Two towers stand on the seaward side of St Aubin's Road, First Tower, which has given its name to the surrounding district, and Beaumont Tower (third tower). The second tower, which stood at Bel Royal, was destroyed during the

German Occupation. At one time First Tower was surmounted by a windmill and cistern, installed to provide water for watering the trees along Victoria Avenue. These excrescences have long since gone and to-day the tower serves as a sewer vent.

Situated at the foot of the southern extremity of Noirmont Headland, just above the sea, is La Tour de Vinde, a tower in the second group, erected some time between 1810 and 1814, probably in 1811. It is now painted black and white and serves as a sea-mark.

To the west of Noirmont on the Ile au Guerdain in Portelet Bay stands another tower in the second group built in 1808. Sometimes the islet is referred to as Janvrin's Tomb because Captain Philip Janvrin was buried there temporarily in 1721 after dying of the plague aboard his ship.

At Ouaisné Bay stands another tower (St Brelade No. 1) and in St Brelade's Bay is yet another (St Brelade No. 2). There are two towers bordering St Ouen's Bay, both of the English pattern, Kempt Tower (St Ouen No. 2) (1834), to the north of L'Ouzière Slipway, and Lewis Tower (St Ouen No. 1) (1835 – builder John Gruchy), near Les Laveurs Slipway, named respectively after Sir James Kempt, Master-General of the Ordnance (1834–38), and Colonel G.G. Lewis, the Commanding Officer of the Royal Engineers in Jersey at that time. The new North Battery comprising three granite gun positions for 32-pounder cannons found on the seaward side of Kempt Tower was probably constructed at the same time as the tower. The Germans added a concrete arched entrance way to the landward side of Lewis Tower. High Tower (St Ouen No. 3, formerly designated St Ouen D) and the tower at L'Etacq (probably 1834 – builder John Benest) were both destroyed during the German Occupation. Nothing remains of three other towers (St Ouen A, B and C), which pre-dated Kempt Tower and Lewis Tower. Between towers C and D was located the Middle Battery to which La Caumine à Mary Best, a small stone building with a high pitched roof, also of stone, served as a magazine. To-day it is painted white and does duty as a sea-mark.

Standing out in St Ouen's Bay is La Rocco Tower (1796–

1801), originally called Fort Gordon after Lieutenant-General Sir H.M. Gordon, the Lieutenant-Governor. When it was completed it consisted of a tower of the Jersey 'martello' design surrounded by a platform with a wall, originally for a battery of five guns. It was used for target practice by the Germans during the Occupation and as a result was extensively damaged. In time it would have been totally destroyed by the sea had it not been for a valiant restoration effort.

At Grève de Lecq, on the north coast, is yet another tower (about 1780). From there until St Martin is reached on the east side of the island there are no more towers. At Fliquet stands a tower, generally referred to as the Telegraph Tower, and at St Catherine's there is another. At Archirondel is a tower (1793–94) surrounded by a platform with a wall, originally for a battery of four guns. Nowadays it is painted red and white and serves as a shipping mark and an adventure training centre. The Victoria Tower (1837) stands on the landward side of the St Catherine's Road near Geoffrey's Leap. Over the door is a stone inscribed "VR 1837". The building is surrounded by a narrow moat. On top of the tower is a telescope used by the Victoria College Astronomical Group.

There are five towers bordering the Royal Bay of Grouville as follows: No. 5, No. 4 (Fauvic), No. 3 (Le Hurel), No. 2 (Keppel Tower), and No. 1 (La Rocque), and there is another at Platte Rocque. Nothing remains of No. 6 which stood to the north of Fort William. There is a building annexed to La Rocque Tower called Le Corps de Garde et Magazin de St Samson.

Standing about a mile and a quarter out in the Royal Bay of Grouville is Seymour Tower built on a rock called L'Avarison. Although the building dates from 1782 its name is probably derived from an earlier tower or fortification built about 1540 and called after Edward Seymour, Duke of Somerset, Governor of Jersey (1537–50). The tower is square and thus differs from all the other Jersey towers of the same period.

At Le Hocq is yet another tower (before 18 June 1781), now the headquarters of the Jersey Amateur Radio Society. On an islet in St Clement's Bay, about two miles from the shore, stands Icho Tower (1810–11), a tower in the second group. Finally, there is La Collette Tower (1834 – by Philip de la Mare), Pointe-des-Pas, St Helier, a tower in the third group.

Other small fortifications around the coast, which formed part of the defences against Napoleon, are: La Tour Carrée (1778) to the north of L'Ouzière Slipway, St Ouen's Bay; the remains of the Leicester Battery, with the ruins of Les Hurets Magazine close by, on the west side of Bouley Bay, Trinity; L'Etacquerel Fort (after 1786 and before 1790) on the east side of the same bay; Fort William or Prince William's Redoubt situated beside Grouville Bay, to the south of Gorey, and Fort Henry or the Square Fort (built some time between 1772 and 1792) also situated beside the bay to the south of Fort William.

FORT REGENT (1806–14 – by John Hambly Humfrey), named after the Prince Regent, situated on the Town Hill, St Helier, is a substantial fortification built at the very end of the Napoleonic Wars (its Guernsey equivalent was Fort George). The foundation stone above the internal arch of the main entrance was laid on 7 November 1806 by Lieutenant-General Don, Lieutenant-Governor. The keystone to the external arch of the main entrance is carved with the cypher of King George III and the date 1806. The fort is coffin shaped and consists of a large parade ground (now roofed over) enclosed by ramparts, northern redoubts, east bastion, west bastion, counterguard and glacis. The well, which still exists, is over two hundred feet deep. The signal post, a feature of the fort, presents an attractive sight especially when dressed overall. It is the successor of the original signal post erected on the Town Hill at the beginning of the eighteenth century.

Some military buildings dating from the nineteenth century are: Rozel Barracks (now Le Couperon Hotel) (1809–10), Rozel Bay; Grève de Lecq Barracks (about 1815), Grève de Lecq, St Mary, comprising the officers' quarters, (now the Grève de Lecq Hotel) and the barracks, now belonging to The National Trust for Jersey and recently restored. At the latter is a rain-water tank bearing the arms of the Board of Ordnance, the letters "B.O", the broad arrow and the date

1832; La Crête Fort (1835) standing at the eastern extremity of Bonne Nuit Bay has a stone roof, and now serves as a country retreat for the Lieutenant-Governor.

There were also six militia arsenals: Town, Grouville, St Lawrence, St Martin, St Mary and St Peter. St Mary's arsenal has been demolished, the remainder have been converted to other uses. The Town Arsenal (1912–13) is now a fire station.

GERMAN FORTIFICATIONS form part of the local scene, which is not surprising considering that Jersey together with the other Channel Islands formed part of Hitler's Western Wall. Three of the most outstanding are the observation towers located respectively at Noirmont and La Corbière, St Brelade, and Les Landes, St Ouen. At Noirmont there are also the German Command Bunker and the Batterie Lothringen. The Corbière observation tower now houses Jersey Radio, which transmits information to local shipping.

GERMAN UNDERGROUND HOSPITAL, St Peter's Valley, was built by the German Todt Organization during the Occupation, and is hewn out of solid rock and covers four acres. It took two and a half years to construct and was fully equipped at the time of the Liberation in 1945.

7

The Fortifications of Guernsey and Alderney

CASTLE CORNET stands on an islet on the south side of St Peter Port Harbour. It was used as a fortification from its inception until 1946 and was added to and altered to meet changing requirements. It has been suggested that the original castle was built between approximately 1206 and 1252. It was strengthened during the French occupation of 1338–45 and again between 1535–46. The keep was destroyed by lightning in 1672.

The main or outer gate of the castle is on the sea side of the town bastion and is reached from the southern arm of the harbour. Immediately above the gateway are the arms of Queen Elizabeth I and higher up are two gunports. Inside is a curved passage, with an inner portcullis, leading to the outer bailey. There on the left is to be found the saluting battery armed with a number of interesting old cannons. On the right are the four bronze plaques from Admiral Lord de Saumarez's obelisk destroyed by the Germans on 7 December 1943, the main guard (about 1750), now containing the Maritime Museum, a gallery of local paintings, the German Occupation Museum, a display of decorations and medals, a display of military equipment and shooting trophies and the Brenner Collection of water-colours by Peter Le Lièvre. Further along on the same side is the guardroom, built of brick and dating from the nineteenth century, now the museum of 201 Squadron Royal Air Force. Ahead is the outer curtain wall pierced by a gateway above which are the arms of Queen Elizabeth II commemorating her visit to the castle in 1957. The next part of the castle to be reached is the barbican with the curtain battery, from which the noon-day gun is fired, around on the left, keeping to the seaward side of the outer

bailey the royal or east battery is passed on the left, then the
married quarters (1745–50) on the right and Hart's battery on
the left. The next section of the outer bailey is reached
through a gateway. It also has two batteries, both on the
seaward side, each with its magazine up against the wall of the
citadel. The first is the well battery and the second, at the southern extremity of the castle, is the south or water battery.
The outer bailey then returns northwards to the Mewtis
bulwark with the inner bailey beyond.

The inner bailey has at its western extremity the western
bastion. Proceeding eastwards the Mewtis bulwark is passed
on the right and then the Carey Tower (1435–37) followed by
the hospital (1746), now used to house the splendid Militia
Museum and the Spencer Militia Collection, with another
building behind containing the armoury. Nearby is the
Sutler's House (1600) with its garden, brilliant in summer-
time, whence it is possible to ascend to the old town jail and
the top of the barbican with its splendid view over the harbour
and the town, or to descend to the prisoners' walk.

During the Occupation the Germans built gun emplace-
ments at the castle and made other additions to the building.

Castle Cornet, like Mont Orgueil Castle and Elizabeth
Castle in Jersey, is floodlit during the summer months.

LE CHATEAU DES MARAIS is a fortification dating from the
early part of the thirteenth century, standing on a hill near
Belle Grève Bay, St Peter Port. It covers an area of about
four acres. It had a wide outer bailey surrounded by a wall
and an inner bailey which had a wall and ditch. Within the
castle stands an eighteenth-century magazine and a German
bunker dating from the Occupation. There was also a building, possibly a chapel, within the walls built during the thirteenth century and destroyed early in the following century.

VALE CASTLE (variously known as Le Château du Valle, St
Michael's Castle and the Castle of the Archangel) with its
impressive gateway stands on the north side of St Sampson's
Harbour, Vale. It is of considerable antiquity, and has been
used as a fortification down the centuries. Even the Germans

made use of it during the Occupation.

TOWERS. Fifteen small round towers were built along the coastline of the island between 1783 and 1787.

The Guernsey towers are built of stone with vertical walls pierced by two rows of loopholes. At the base they measure 20 feet across and their walls are 4 feet thick. They were considered unsatisfactory and their guns were never mounted.

Tower No. 1 which stood at Hougue à la Perre was demolished in 1905 and Tower No. 2 which stood near the top of Victoria Avenue at Les Banques suffered the same fate in 1959. Tower No. 3 stands on Mont Crevelt, St Sampson. Towers Nos. 4–7 inclusive are to be found at intervals on the coastal side of L'Ancresse Common. Towers Nos. 9, 10 and 11 are located respectively at Baie de la Jaonneuse, Chouet and Rousse, Vale. Towers Nos 12, 13, 14 and 15 are located respectively at Vazon Road, Castel, Petit Bôt, Forest, Saints Bay, St Martin and Fermain Bay, St Peter Port.

In addition to its ancient castles and its 'martello' towers, Guernsey has a large number of fortifications and related buildings in varying states of preservation, including: the remains of Clarence Battery, Le Coquelin (The Pepper Pot), a circular look-out, and nearby powder magazine and gun platform, all at Fermain Point, St Peter Port; Bec du Nez Battery and Magazine and Saints Bay Right Battery and Magazine, St Martin's; the Magazine at Les Sommeilleuses, Forest, Mont Hérault Watch House, St Peter's; Fort Pezeries, Pezeries Point, Torteval; Fort Grey (now Fort Grey Maritime Museum) (Le Château de Rocquaine or 'The Cup and Saucer'), St Peter's, erected in 1804 on the site of an earlier fortification and restored in 1975 as a museum of shipwrecks, which was most appropriate as it stands within sight of treacherous reefs where many ships have foundered; Brock Battery, L'Erée Point Battery, Fort Sausmarez, heightened by the Germans during the Occupation, and Magazine, all also in St Peter's; Fort Richmond, St Saviour's; Fort Hommet at the north end of Vazon Bay, Castel; Mont Cuet Watch House, Vale; Fort Pembroke on the west side of L'Ancresse Bay, Vale; Fort Le Marchant (the Victorian barracks were demolished in 1971) on the east side of L'Ancresse Bay; Fort Doyle, between Banque Mouton and Fontaine-ès-Boeufs, Vale; the Bréhon Tower (1856) on a rock in the Little Russel, half way between Guernsey and Herm.

GERMAN FORTIFICATIONS form part of the local scene as they do in Jersey. Two of the most outstanding are the range-finder post at L'Angle, Torteval, and the observation and range-finding tower at Pleinmont in the same parish.

THE GERMAN UNDERGROUND HOSPITAL, La Vassalerie, St Andrew's, is similar to that in Jersey and, like its counterpart, was built by the Todt Organization. It took approximately three and a half years to build and covers an area of about 75,000 square feet, with a mile and a quarter of corridors and rooms. The hospital was excavated from solid rock, it being estimated that some 60,000 tons were removed during its construction. It was completed in 1944 and was only used to accommodate German troops wounded in France fighting the allied forces.

Few places of its size can have as many fortifications as Alderney.

THE NUNNERY, situated close by the shore at Longy Bay, is undoubtedly the oldest fortification in the island. Some believe it to be a late Roman fort built in the latter half of the fourth century; others that it is of more recent date. The building originally consisted of a square enclosure with rounded corners, surrounded by curtain walls with a bastion at each corner. At some time long ago a large part of the east wall and a small par of the south wall together with the south-east bastion collapsed. A wall was built to replace them from the east end of the remaining south wall running northwards towards the north wall and then returning eastwards to join the remaining south end of the east wall. The walls are between 4½ and 5 feet thick at the base and between 16½ and 18 feet high. All but the west wall has a parapet 5 feet high and a rampart-walk about 3 feet wide. The first section of each bastion is solid up to the height of 10 feet; the upper 5 feet section is hollowed out to form a recess. The entrance to the building is through a gateway in the north wall. Within the enclosure backing against the west wall is a house with two windows cut through the wall. During the Occupation the Germans re-fortified the place and converted it into a communications centre. A machine-gun post was created in the south-west bastion and another was built on top of the north-west bastion.

ESSEX CASTLE or ESSEX FORT above Longy Bay was built in the sixteenth century; work was probably started in 1546 and ceased in 1554 before it was fully completed. The attractive watch-tower or gazebo was built by John Le Mesurier between 1812 and 1818. The present building incorporating part of the original castle was built in the nineteenth century along with the general fortifications of the island. During the early years of the present century it was used as a military hospital and has now been converted into flats.

Around the coast of Alderney are a number of fortifications dating from the nineteenth century built by the British Government alarmed at the fortifications and harbour being built by the French at Cherbourg. This alarm seems particularly extraordinary considering that France was Great Britain's ally in the Crimea War (1854–55).

Starting at the west end of the north coast of the island, to the west of Braye Harbour, and moving eastwards the fortifications are as follows: Fort Clonque (1853–possibly 1855), reached by a causeway, and Fort Tourgis (about 1855), the second largest fort in the island, both overlooking the Swinge; Fort Platte Saline (about 1855) at Saline Bay; Fort Doyle (about 1855) at Crabby Bay and Fort Grosnez (1847–52) at the landward end of the Breakwater; Fort Albert (originally called Fort Touraille), the largest fort in the island, standing on Mont Touraille and commanding the entrance to Braye Harbour with Roselle Battery below and the Arsenal protected by Mount Hale Fort to the south; Château l'Etoc (1853) on the headland with Dunnette Bay to the west and Arch Bay to the east, now converted into flats; Fort Corblets (1852), with Corblets Bay to the west and Vaux Trembliers Bay to the east, now a private house; Fort Houmeaux Florains (1854); Fort Quesnard (1853) and Fort Houmet Herbé (possibly 1854), at the eastern extremity of the island; Fort Ile de Raz (possibly 1854), reached by a fine causeway from the road bordering the south side of Longy Common, and now converted into flats; Frying Pan Battery, on the coast below Essex Castle.

THE TELEGRAPH TOWER, Telegraph Bay, as its name indicates, was built as a signal station in the early years of the nineteenth century and now does duty as a sea-mark.

THE GERMAN FORTIFICATIONS are still much in evidence in Alderney as it was very strongly fortified during the Occupation. Three relics from those sad days in the island's history are Batterie Annes on the heights of La Giffoine on the west coast, Les Mouriaux Water Tower, St Anne, and the heavy flak battery at Mannez Garenne on the east coast.

Greenhill, St Peter, Jersey – the best example of an untouched seventeenth-century frontage in the island

Double arch entrance to Hamptonne Farm, St Lawrence, Jersey

Quetivel Mill, St Peter, Jersey – its restoration by The National Trust for Jersey earned a commendation in the 1978 Civic Trust Awards

La Haye du Puits, Castel, Guernsey

The unicorn and the greyhound, supporters of the de Sausmarez Arms carved by Sir Henry Cheere, Bt., adorning the entrance of Sausmarez Manor, St Martin's, Guernsey
(*Below left*) Exterior and (*below right*) interior of the dovecot at Torteval, Guernsey

Les Niots Mill, Les Niaux, Talbot Valley, Castel, Guernsey

La Seigneurie, Sark

The dovecot at La Seigneurie, Sark

The lighthouse at Mannez, Alderney

The prison, Herm

The unveiling of the Don Monument, The Parade, St Helier, Jersey, in 1885

8

The Towns of St Helier and St Aubin

ST HELIER has always been the capital of Jersey. The Town, as it is often called, stands on the south coast of the island and occupies a low-lying site within a semicircle of hills. Looking at the town from the sea there is to be seen the harbour, flanked on its western side by Elizabeth Castle, the Hermitage Rock and the Breakwater and on its eastern side by the Town Hill, on which stands Fort Regent, now converted into a leisure centre, and the electricity power-station with its tall chimney; in the middle distance, looking from west to east, are the white bulk of West Park Pavilion, standing out against the green slopes of Westmount, the Grand Hotel, and then the miscellaneous line of buildings which borders the Esplanade. Further in the distance is the mass of the town from which little can be distinguished except the spires of St Thomas's and St Mark's Churches and a number of tall modern blocks, with high up in the background, Almorah Crescent and over to the east the main block of Victoria College.

St Helier is very ancient, although it is impossible to say with any certainty how old it is. One writer states that it was first mentioned in the Assize Roll of 1299, but undoubtedly it existed long before then, even if only as little more than a village. It remained of small extent for many centuries and certainly until well into the seventeenth century it covered only a long narrow area bordered by King Street and Queen Street on the north and Broad Street and Hill Street on the south. On the east it extended as far as La Motte Street and on the west to Charing Cross. It should be mentioned that those thoroughfares were not so named at that time. During the eighteenth century the town underwent some development.

Peter Meade's map of 1737 shows limited expansion on both the east and west sides and M. Momonier's map of 1787 shows further extensions and consolidation. During the following century the town underwent considerable further development as is clearly shown by a comparison of Elias Le Gros's map of 1834 with Albert Francis Grellier's of 1904. Between 1800 and 1914 the area of the town was multiplied many times and suburbs grew up, notably Cheapside, First Tower, Rouge Bouillon, Havre des Pas, Georgetown and St Luke's, extending in the last two cases beyond the parish boundaries.

St Helier began to develop with greater rapidity from the beginning of the nineteenth century, the expansion gaining momentum after the end of the Napoleonic Wars in 1815, when a number of retired naval and army officers as well as people from other parts of the British Isles and France settled in the island, many of them in the town.

The first major development was the removal of the market from what is now the Royal Square to where the main section of the Central Market now stands and the building of the west side of Halkett Place on the site of Government House and its garden. The expansion then moved north, east and west, ultimately reaching on the north from west to east, Upper King's Cliff, Almorah Cemetery, Richmond Road, Almorah Crescent and Victoria Crescent; on the east, from north to south, Trinity Road, Springfield Road, the foot of St Saviour's Hill, St Saviour's Road, Pleasant Street, Clarence Road, Don Road, Georgetown, St Luke's and St Clement's Road as far as Marine Terrace (partly demolished 1978) and the Victoria Baths Hotel (demolished 1978); on the west, from north to south Queen's Road, Undercliff Road, St John's Road and Peirson Road.

Within that approximate area a 'New Town' was built containing every type of dwelling from substantial houses standing in their own grounds, fine crescents, terraces and rows of substantial houses to modest houses and single-storey cottages. Shops were also built to serve the new districts that had grown up. At the end of this great period of expansion St Helier compared favourably with any town of similar size in England or elsewhere.

With the passing of the years further consolidation and expansion took place. The growth of the tourist industry which had started with the coming of peace to Europe in 1815 and with improved sea communications resulted in the building of hotels and the conversion of houses into guest-houses to cater for the increasing number of visitors.

Since the ending of World War II in 1945 St Helier has expanded still further and in recent years because the island has become a banking and financial centre of some importance an appreciable number of new banks and finance houses have opened, many of them with first-rate premises.

To-day such old buildings and 'character' as St Helier possesses remains within the 'Old Town' limits, notably in the Royal Square and the thoroughfares in the near vicinity. The square served as a market-place until 1800 when a new market was built where the present Central Market now stands. To-day it is paved with granite and has horse-chestnut trees along its north and south sides. The buildings around the square are of no great architectural merit or beauty yet collectively they form an attractive group.

A range of public buildings containing from east to west the States' Chamber, Public Registry, Royal Court House, Judicial Greffe, Public Library and States' Offices forms the south side of the square.

The building (by W.J. Ancell & James Orange) containing the States' Chamber adjoins the east side of the Royal Court House. It also contains on the ground floor, beneath the chamber, the strong-rooms of the Public Registry. The strong-rooms were opened in 1879 and the States' Chamber on 21 July 1887 when the States voted a loyal address to Queen Victoria on the occasion of her Golden Jubilee. The public entrance to the States' Chamber is in Halkett Place. The interior of the chamber is in early Jacobean style. The ceiling, which is divided into nine large panels, is carved and panelled, and moulded in Parian cement. It is supported by twelve pilasters on each of which is a large shield. It is covered with wood framing and glazed with stained glass. The floor of the House is horseshoe shaped with the dais for the Bailiff and Lieutenant-Governor at the open west end. The dais, desks and seats are of carved oak. The seats for the members are upholstered in red leather and so arranged in tiers and placed that each member has an uninterrupted view of the President, whose seat is raised slightly above that of the Lieutenant-Governor. The enclosure of the room is also of oak up to gallery level and is carved and panelled and was decorated with hand-painted Tynecastle. The latter has been replaced by red leather panels each with the arms of the island embossed in gold at its centre. At the east end there is a members' lobby. Over the doorway facing the dais is carved the motto *'Dieu et mon droit'*. There is a distinguished visitors' gallery, a public gallery, two nominally private galleries and a Press box. There is a tablet on the wall to the memory of Sir Walter Ralegh, Governor of Jersey (1600–1603), erected in 1920 by La Société Jersiaise. Affixed to the front of the canopy over the President's and the Lieutenant-Governor's chairs is a staff from which hangs a banner of the arms of Jersey, designed by N.V.L. Rybot and executed by the Royal School of Needlework for the visit of King George V, Queen Mary and Princess Mary in 1921. The States' Chamber was renovated in 1965, and microphones were installed in 1966. The Silver Jubilee portrait of Queen Elizabeth II (1979 – by Norman Hepple) hangs at the entrance to the chamber.

The Royal Court House has occupied its present site on the southern side of the Royal Square since time immemorial. In 1309 the house in which the King's Pleas were held was restored at a cost of twenty sols. Since then the court house has been rebuilt and reconstructed on a number of occasions. The present building dates from 1866. Above the entrances facing the square are the coats of arms of King George VI (bailiff's entrance) and King George II (public entrance). The former commemorates the visit of King George VI and Queen Elizabeth on 7 June 1945 and was unveiled by the present Queen (then Princess Elizabeth) in 1957: the latter is particularly fine and was originally over the entrance of the Court House completed in 1769. There are marks cut into the pavement bordering the front of the Royal Court House and the Public Registry against which surveyors and conveyancing clerks are able to check the accuracy of their measuring tapes.

The Bailiff's Chambers and the Court Room are on the first floor of the building. On the staircase giving access to the former hangs a painting (1979 – by Ken Howard) depicting the interior of the States' Chamber on the occasion of the visit of the Queen and Prince Philip in 1978; let into the wall at the top of the staircase giving access to the latter is a brass strip which is the standard *mesure de verge*, one Imperial yard.

The Court Room is divided into sections. The seats for the bailiff, the lieutenant-governor (when he attends) and the jurats are raised above the body of the court. There are seats for the law officers, the viscount, the advocates and solicitors, and the lords of the manor. There is also a public gallery. The well of the court is covered in carpet of the same colour as the bailiff's robe. The seats occupied by the bailiff and the lieutenant-governor are said to be Tudor. Above them is a wooden canopy incorporating a carving of the royal arms by Henry William Sohièr (born 1827), who much to his disgust received the sum of only £55 for the work, £17 less than the amount for which he asked.

On the ceiling are painted the names of a number of persons most of whom wrote either on Norman or Jersey law. Those whose names appear are: André, Basnage, Bérault, d'Argenté, d'Aviron, Hr. de Carteret, Godefroi, Jn. Herault, Le Geyt, Le Rouillé, Poingdestre and Terrien. Guillaume Le Rouillé wrote a commentary on *Le Grand Coutumier du Pays et Duché de Normandie* published in 1534. H. Basnage, J. Bérault and J. Godefroi (with others) each wrote a commentary on *La Coutume Réformée* of Normandy, published respectively 1678–81, in 1614 and in 1626. Helier de Carteret and John Herault were both Bailiffs of Jersey, the former 1513–14, 1516–23 and 1529–61 and the latter 1615–21 and 1624–26. Philip Le Geyt was Lieutenant-Bailiff 1729–47 and wrote a number of works on Jersey law. John Poingdestre was Lieutenant-Bailiff 1669–76 and also wrote a number of works on Jersey law. G. Terrien wrote *Commentaires du droit civil tant public que privé, observé au pays et duché de Normandie*, published 1574–78.

The Court Room contains an interesting collection of paintings including King George III by Philip Jean (1755–1802), a

Jersey artist. Field Marshal Henry Seymour Conway, Governor of Jersey (1772–95), by Thomas Gainsborough; *The Death of Major Peirson* (a copy painted in 1866 by W. Holyoake from the original by John Singleton Copley in the Tate Gallery, London); Francis Godfray and Peter Le Sueur, both by W.M. Hay; Sir William Henry Venables Vernon, Bailiff of Jersey (1899–1931), and *Assize of Heritage* both by John St Helier Lander; Lord Coutanche, Bailiff of Jersey (1935–61), and Cecil Stanley Harrison, Bailiff of Jersey (1961–62), both by Sir James Gunn. King George "as a particular mark of condescension and favour, agreed to give Mr. Jean one sitting to enable him to finish the picture". When *The Death of Major Peirson* came up for auction in 1864, the States authorized the Bailiff, John Hammond, to attend the sale in London and to bid for it up to the sum of £1,000. The States were outbid and were so disappointed at losing the picture that they commissioned Holyoake to make a copy. In the painting the statue of King George II is clearly visible above the smoke of gunfire.

The Public Library (1886 – by Ancell & Orange) was built on the site of the Union Hotel. On the wall of the staircase giving access to the library is a marble memorial to Philip Falle (1656–1742), the founder of the library, and over the mantelpiece inside the library is a portrait of him (artist not known), removed there from the original library in 1886. Beneath the library are the offices of the Judicial Greffe and the Old Committee Room. On the north wall of the passage between the General Office and the Old Committee Room hang two portraits, one of Falle and one of Dr Daniel Dumaresq (1712–1805), a benefactor of the Public Library. It was in the Old Committee Room in February 1941 that the Germans tried sixteen young Frenchmen who escaped from France in a boat and were captured as they were landing in Guernsey thinking it was the Isle of Wight. One of them, François Scornet, assumed responsibility for the escape and was condemned to death (*see* Chapter 10) and the remainder were sentenced to terms of imprisonment.

The States Building (1931 – by Roy Blampied) with its entrance on to Church Street (La Rue du Trousse Cotillon or 'Tuck-up-your-petticoat Street') completes the block. It is partly faced with granite and bears in Roman numerals high up on its western front the date of its erection. At the centre of the parapet on the west side are carved a pair of entwined dolphins. On the north-west corner of the building are carved the arms of Jersey with those of Sir William Vernon, Bailiff, beneath; on the south-west corner are carved the arms of Charles Edward Malet de Carteret, Bailiff 1931–35. The two portraits hanging on the wall of the staircase inside the main entrance are of King James II and his second wife, Mary of Modena.

The Old Corn Market (1671) occupies the west side of the Royal Square. Inside the bank which now occupies the ground floor of the building are the granite arches of the original market. The upper part of the building at one time contained an assembly room where John Wesley preached in 1787. High up on the east frontage of the building are the Royal Arms and the arms of Jersey.

Nearby stands the picket house (1803) with a colonnade (1835). The drainheads on the north and south sides of the building bear the cypher of King George III. The sundial on the south wall was erected by the parish.

The square is bordered on its north side by Vine Street (La Rue des Vignes). Opposite the picket house are Nos. 1 and 2, now occupied by a stationers and formerly the York Hotel. The building has a passageway through its centre, giving access to King Street. The buildings immediately to the east are more or less similar and must have been built about the same time. The surrounds of the windows are of dressed granite. The shop forming the corner of Vine Street and Peirson Place, occupied by a jeweller's, bears a firemark (1747) on the side facing the square and retains its wooden exterior shutters which when in place completely enclose the shop windows. This type of shutter was at one time common in the town, but has now almost disappeared. However, it so happens that the jeweller's shop at the north-east corner of Peirson Place also has the same type of shutters.

Peirson Place must be the shortest thoroughfare in the town. The hero's surname appears as 'Peirson' on the nameplate at the Royal Square end and as 'Pierson' on the nameplate at the King Street end. On the west side of the street is a delightful little building, originally a house, and now forming the back part of the first jeweller's mentioned above. On the east side is The Peirson public house (*see* below), fronting onto the square. The building probably dates from 1745, the date on the drainheads, and at one time was a bookshop. Both it and the building across the street (the jeweller's on the corner) are depicted in the painting *The Death of Major Peirson*. On the gable of the Peirson giving on to Peirson Place are black spots supposedly marking the places where shots hit the building during the Battle of Jersey.

Two buildings form the east side of the square, The Cosy Corner public house (*see* below) and the Chamber of Commerce building. On the east frontage of the latter is reproduced the seal of the Chamber, the oldest Chamber of Commerce in the English-speaking world, founded on 28 February 1768.

Off the north-west corner of the Royal Square is Library Place where stands the original brick-built library (1737–41 – by J.H. Bastide) from which the thoroughfare takes its name. The top storey of the building was added in 1820. The drainheads bear the initials "P.F." (for Philip Falle) and the date "1736". The interior of the building, although much altered, has a staircase with heavy turned balusters and a wide flat-topped handrail, and the entrance doorway to the first-floor room, which housed the library, has deeply moulded architraves and a heavy pediment. No. 7 Library Place, which stands next door to the old library is an attractive modern building occupied by a travel agent.

On the opposite side of the road No. 8 Library Place (Middle section 1864: first extension 1900 – by Adolphus Curry) is a bank, successor to the Channel Islands Bank. The western end of the building has a clock tower surmounted by a copper dome. The building covers the site of the premises where lived Pierre Emile Langelier for whose death Madeleine Smith stood trial for murder. He was born close by in Vine Street. On the same side of the street, to the west, at the corner of New Cut, is No. 16 Library Place (west section 1874 – by Hayward & Son: second section 1932: third section

1962) also a bank. The oldest part of the premises was originally occupied by the Jersey Commercial Bank (Robin Bros.), founded 1808 and taken over by Parr's Bank in 1908. The west end and centre of the premises are in the Venetian Gothic style and are built of red granite with soft stone dressings. The arms of Jersey are carved on the stonework above the main entrance.

Library Place leads into Broad Street (La Grande Rue), originally the principal thoroughfare of the town. A sea wall stretches at the rear of the premises on the south side of Broad Street from about the post office past Castle Street but it has been hidden from view for many years and is exposed only when building works are carried out from time to time. At the western end of the street is Charing Cross (La Pompe de Bas) where the prison spanned the street until the new prison was built in Gloucester Street in 1811. The prison marked the western limit of the town except for a few streets, Old Street (Le Vieux Chemin), Hue Street (La Rue de Hue or La Rue de la Poste) and Dumaresq Street built during the eighteenth century.

At Charing Cross stands La Croix de la Reine (1977 – designed by C. Warren), a granite cross carved with the following motifs: St Helier's Parish Church, Elizabeth Castle, St Helier's Hermitage, Old Prison, the Town Hill, St Helier, an ormer shell, a town pump, the gold torque, a sailing ship, a Jersey milkcan, "V" for *Vega* (the name of the Red Cross ship which brought supplies to the Channel Islands towards the end of the German Occupation) or Victory, the Queen's Silver Jubilee Emblem, the arms of the parish of St Helier and an inscription stating that the cross was a gift from the trustees of the Town Vingtaine. On her visit to Jersey in 1978 the Queen accepted a book about the cross from the parish of St Helier. It was presented to her at the cross by the Constable (Mayor), as was a red white and blue heart by a pupil from one of the island's kindergartens.

Charing Cross merges into York Street where the Town Hall (1872 – by Le Sueur & Brée: 1966–67 – reconstruction by Le Sueur & Baker) stands at the corner of Seale Street. The building contains a hall where parish assemblies and other functions are held, the municipal offices and the police court (1901 – by Percy A. Aubin). The parish, in addition to its ancient records, owns a collection of municipal plate and chains of office, as well as a number of pictures, including *La Repasseuse* (The Ironer) by Jacques Louis David, which hangs in the Constable's Room.

Along Broad Street, on the south side, going eastwards from the cross, are a number of buildings worth noting or buildings with features worth noting. Inside No. 31 is preserved a stone carved with the initials "FDPL" and "PG" and the date "1673". No. 15 is the post office (1909: modernized 1972 – by B.J.R. Garner & Associates) which incorporates the Philatelic Bureau, and bears on its exterior the cypher of King Edward VII. The post office which it replaced still exists in Halkett Place and is now used as a club. No. 13 is a bank with a date stone on its frontage inscribed, "PML MC 1762". The initials are those of Pierre Mallet and his first wife Marie Chepmell. The building was splendidly reconstructed (1970 – by B.J.R. Garner & Associates) by its present occupiers and inside are to be seen some fine examples of modern craftsmanship. No. 9 (1858 – by Philip Brée; 1963 – extension on the Conway Street side) forms the corner of Broad Street and Conway Street and is occupied by yet another bank. Originally it was the premises of the Jersey Joint Stock Bank (Arthur, de Carteret & Co.). The large building at the east end of the street, forming the corner of Library Place and facing the Le Sueur obelisk, is now a bank but from 1810 until it was closed in 1969 was the British Hotel.

At the south-east end of Broad Street, across Conway Street, is Bond Street, a pleasant thoroughfare with a Georgian aspect, although many of the properties have been rebuilt or reconstructed over the years. No. 2 has a fine doorcase, No. 3 retains its old shop front, No. 4 has granite dressings as well as an attractive doorcase, No. 5 is the headquarters of the local branch of the Royal Air Force Association and a plaque on its exterior records its opening as such by Air Chief Marshal The Earl of Bandon in 1964, and No. 8 has a firemark, once affixed to the outside and now preserved inside.

In Pier Road is the Museum of La Société Jersiaise, the

local antiquarian society, occupying an excellent example of a merchant's house, built for Philip Nicolle in about 1815. The splendid extension (1977–78) occupies the site of No. 7 Pier Road and reproduces the frontage of that building, except that a window has been substituted for the front door.

The two main inner routes through the town from east to west are La Motte Street, Queen Street and King Street (the two latter thoroughfares are now for pedestrians only) passing to the north of the Royal Square and joining the west end of Broad Street at Charing Cross, and Colomberie, Hill Street and Mulcaster Street passing to the south of the Royal Square.

La Motte Street runs from the north end of St James's Street to Queen Street. On the corner of St James's Street and Grosvenor Street stood the La Maison de la Motte, the home of Major Moses Corbet, Lieutenant-Governor at the time of the Battle of Jersey (1781), at the eastern limit of the 'Old Town'. On the north side of La Motte Street, towards its eastern end, stands all that remains of Hemery Row (built by James Hemery, died 1831), an early very dignified terrace of houses, originally with small front gardens enclosed by railings. The stone bearing the initials "ILT" and "FLT" and the date "1699" from No. 15, has been preserved and incorporated in the development (1976) which covers the site.

Queen Street (probably named after Queen Charlotte, the consort of King George III, and previously called either La Rue du Milieu or La Rue-ès-Porcqs), now a pedestrian precinct, runs from La Motte Street westwards to King Street. It contains few buildings of interest beyond The Exeter (*see* below) and Queensway House, a pleasing development incorporating a stone inscribed "IH 1751" above the entrance to the arcade.

King Street (probably named after King George III and previously called La Rue Derrière), now a pedestrian precinct, runs westwards to Charing Cross. The building occupied by a branch of a well-known multiple tailors has two foundation stones, one on the Halkett Place side inscribed "THIS STONE LAID BY ARNOLD JAMES BURTON 1932" and one on the King Street side inscribed "THIS STONE LAID BY STANLEY HOWARD BURTON 1932". Next door is a branch of another multiple store which occupies the site of the Lieutenant-Governor's residence from 1800 until 1822. The shop on the opposite side of the road with a granite upper storey was built in 1786. No. 35 has a pleasing frontage with decorative ironwork running along the top of the shop windows. The premises, No. 36 King Street (1834), on the corner of that thoroughfare and New Street, now a retail wine and spirit shop, were at one time occupied by the Jersey Mercantile Union Bank (Le Bailly, Deslandes & Co.) which accounts for its fine granite frontage. On the same side of the street, going westwards is the King's Arcade (1883 – by Hayward & Sons), part of one of Jersey's leading stores (founded 1810). The King Street entrance to the arcade is of Portland stone and the fine gates were made in Exeter. When the arcade was opened it was lit by the new 'liquid' (electric) light.

Colomberie (at one time called Dove Street) runs from St Clement's Road to Hill Street. It contains little of interest beyond Colomberie House (now a school), once the property of the Hemery family.

Hill Street (formerly called La Rue des Trois Pigeons and before that La Rue de Haut) contains a few interesting buildings. In the façade of No. 35 is a stone inscribed "PH AC 1737". No. 27 was the Grand Hôtel du Calvados and No. 25 was an annexe to the hotel. No. 23 has a pleasing frontage. In the façade of No. 16 is a stone inscribed "IP 1748", the initials standing for 'Jean Perrochon'. The interior has some good features. The property may have been Les Trois Pigeons public house from which the street took the more recent of its old names. The thoroughfare contains many legal offices. The premises Nos. 2 and 4 Hill Street, now solely occupied by a bank, until not many years ago were shared by it with a firm of wine merchants. The bank is the successor to the Channel Islands Bank which in turn was successor to Godfray, Major & Co. (Old Bank, established 1797).

Mulcaster Street (named after Captain F.G. Mulcaster, one of the heroes of the Battle of Jersey) contains little of interest beyond The Grapes public house (*see* below).

The turning to the left at the end of Mulcaster Street is

Caledonia Place. On the corner is the Royal Yacht Hotel (*see* below) and beyond that on the left is the rear entrance of the Jersey Museum consisting of a granite archway with fine wrought-iron gates. Further along the road is the west entrance of the tunnel and beyond that Commercial Buildings (Le Quai des Marchands), which used to be an attractive row of merchants' premises, built between 1818 and 1821, but have been considerably altered with the passing of the years.

The two main outer east–west routes through the town are Springfield Road, Rouge Bouillon, Elizabeth Place, Parade, Gloucester Street (connecting with the Esplanade), or Cheapside and Peirson Road (also connecting with the Esplanade), and La Route du Fort, The Tunnel (1970), Weighbridge and Esplanade.

The Jersey College for Girls (formerly The Jersey Ladies College) (1887–88 – by Adolphus Curry: extensions from 1891–92 to the present day) stands on the north side of Rouge Bouillon (east section). Police Headquarters (1967 – by M. Boots) stands on the east side of Rouge Bouillon (west section) and behind it is the Fire Station (originally the Town Arsenal) (1912–13 – by Edmund Berteau) built of pink granite. The former fire station (1921), off David Place, still exists.

The General Hospital (1860–63 – by Thomas Gallichan), Gloucester Street, replaced the second hospital destroyed by fire in 1859; the original hospital was destroyed, also by fire, in 1783. The present building is of granite and there is a clock (1865) in the pediment of the centre block; above the main entrance is the inscription *"Hôpital Général, Fondé 1767, Reconstruit 1860"*. In front of the main entrance and bordering Gloucester Street is the porter's lodge. The Nurses' Home on the south side of the forecourt was opened in 1950 by the Duchess of Kent. The wing on the north side was opened in 1962; three years earlier Princess Margaret unveiled a commemorative plaque in the building. Funds for the forerunner of the present chapel (*see* Chapter 4) were donated by Charles Robin and his arms are to be seen high up on the north wing of the main hospital building.

The building (1901 – by Adolphus Curry), constructed of

granite, now occupied by the Tourism Committee which forms the corner of the Esplanade and the Weighbridge and faces the car park was the St Helier terminus of the Jersey Railway (J.R. & T.).

The harbour and its vicinity, Snow Hill, Hill Street, Pier Road and Green Street are all dominated by the Town Hill surmounted by Fort Regent (*see* Chapter 6) now a leisure centre. The parade ground has been covered with an undulating roof with a dome at its centre. It is of striking design (by Breakwell and Davies) marred to some extent at its southern end by the fact that the final downturn of the roof (the roof of the swimming pool) is too far removed from the main building, also on its east side by the two tower blocks, La Collette Flats and The Cedars in Green Street. The Leisure Centre may be reached by road, steps, cabin lift and escalator and provides a wide variety of facilities.

The two inner routes through the town from north to south are Val Plaisant, New Street, New Cut, Broad Street and Conway Street, and Midvale Road, David Place and Bath Street. The two outer routes are St Saviour's Road, running from the foot of St Saviour's Hill to the north end of St James's Street, and Queen's Road, Rouge Bouillon (west section) and Elizabeth Place. Whereas the two main inner east–west routes pass through the 'Old Town', the north part of the north–south routes pass through the 'New Town'. Except for the Trustee Savings Bank building (1870) in New Street (La Rue Durell) with its pleasing granite frontage and Nos. 26 and 28, two eighteenth-century houses with granite chimney-stacks, shorn of their front gardens as the result of road widening, none of the buildings in the four north–south routes is of special interest except for those referred to individually elsewhere. The remainder of the buildings in these thoroughfares are covered by the general description of the 'New Town' which follows. In passing it should be mentioned that the row of houses, Nos. 49–55 New Street, used to bear the rather pleasing name of 'Paradise Row'. Philip John Ouless, the artist, lived at No. 53.

The 'New Town' contains many terraces of houses. Some consist of a number of houses in an unbroken row with a carriage drive in front and a grass verge or a shrubbery (in some cases with a few trees) and a wall, sometimes surmounted by iron railings, between it and the road. Examples of this type of terrace are: Almorah Crescent (1844–45) off La Pouquelaye and Victoria Crescent (1854), Upper Midvale Road, The Crescent (sometimes called the Royal Crescent) (1829 or before), Don Road, consisting of two rows of houses with an open space between them, originally occupied by the Theatre Royal (destroyed by fire in 1863). Some terraces have pairs of houses instead of a continuous row. An example of this type of terrace is Windsor Terrace (1835), Val Plaisant, and Don Crescent, off Don Road. Then there are terraces of houses forming one architectural group but with separate front gardens and divided from the road by walls surmounted by iron railings. Such terraces have names but are generally also numbered with the other houses in the street, for example, Peirson Terrace, Havre-des-Pas. In some cases the front door is reached by a flight of granite steps; in others one flight serves two front doors.

There were shops in the 'New Town' to serve the various localities. Many of these premises had attractive shop fronts. Unfortunately, even if the shops have survived for the most part the original shop fronts have been replaced. There were also livery stables to provide carriages for the residents of the 'New Town' and in some cases excursion cars for the visitors, and a number of these premises still survive although vastly changed.

Exterior features to be noted when looking at the houses in the 'New Town' are: fanlights, in the case of the older residences, such as Hemery Row; shutters which are becoming increasingly scarce; window hoods and balconies with ornamental iron work as at Almorah Crescent and at Havre-des-Pas; canopied verandas such as at Peel Terrace, La Route du Fort; classical porches which are to be seen in many terraces and streets. The older houses have substantial granite chimney-stacks.

In passing it should be mentioned that, unlike in the United Kingdom, the iron railings in the Channel Islands survived World War II, although some have been removed since the Liberation.

St Helier has a fine range of covered markets. The New Market (1882 – by Helliwell & Bellamy) in Halkett Place is a splendid example of its type. The roof, which has a large central dome, is made of glass, and supported by iron pillars at the top of some of which are the arms of Jersey in their proper colours. The outer walls dividing the market from Halkett Place and Beresford Street are of fine pinkish granite with wide openings filled with iron railings and gates. The gates at the Hilgrove Lane and Market Street entrances belong to the former pork market, retained when the old market, dating from the beginning of the century, was demolished to make way for its successor. Incorporated in their design are cornucopiae, bunches of grapes, peacocks and the heads of various animals and birds. Beneath the dome is a circular pool with a fountain in the middle comprising three cream-coloured terracotta bowls set one above the other around a central pillar, the smallest at the top and the largest at the bottom. Beneath the rim of the lowest bowl are four cherub-like figures each seated on a jar, lying sideways, and holding a paddle. Encircling the figures, but at a lower level, is a rockery sprouting various types of greenery. The pool contains goldfish. Within the market is a post office (1972 – by Malcolm Peck & Partners) with an old pillar box outside the entrance.

The Beresford Market (1854) running from Beresford Street to Minden Place is devoted to the sale of flowers, fruit, vegetables and fish. It has a pleasant granite frontage on to Beresford Street with the arms of Jersey on the pediment.

St Helier has a great many public houses of which a high proportion are of no special interest. One of the oldest is the granite-built La Folie situated on the land between the English harbour and the French harbour. It probably dates from between 1700 and 1737 although originally it may not have been a public house. Another old licensed house is The Cosy Corner (formerly the Cock and Bottle) with two frontages, both pleasant, one on the Royal Square and the other on Halkett Place. Unfortunately, the little balcony towards the Royal Square is obscured by a sign. Close by is The

Peirson occupying a building probably erected in 1745. On the exterior was painted for many years the simple statement "Here Peirson Fell, 1781", which often drew ribald remarks from visitors and others who knew nothing of Peirson and the battle. The Exeter in Queen Street, is an old public house with a pleasing frontage. It was at one time the starting point for Asplet & Co.'s horsedrawn omnibuses. The Red Lion, Halkett Place, is also an old public house. It retains some engraved glass in its modest but pleasing frontage, but the large wooden red lion which stood on a beam set at a right-angle to the street has long since gone. It was at one time the starting-point of the Caesarean Omnibus Co.'s horsedrawn omnibuses. The Red Lamp on the corner of Peter Street and Ingouville Place bears the date 1846. The Prince of Wales in Hilgrove Street (still referred to by some as French Lane) is said to date from about 1820. It has a fine old frontage with an attractive fanlight over the entrance. The building sports a lamp sign surmounted by a gold crown. The Grapes (for a time known as Daly's) (carving by Jean Philippe Giffard), Mulcaster Street, has a remarkable frontage like one huge sign incorporating bunches of grapes, comic faces, classical figures, pillars and urns, a huge festoon, and an iron balcony with a leaf design, the whole surmounted by a seated figure of Britannia, with shield and trident and behind a flagstaff from which the Union Jack was flown. Unfortunately the frontage has been modified with the passing of the years. However, Britannia survives in all her splendour. The Lillie Langtry, La Motte Street, is a theme house in Victorian style with pictures of the 'Jersey Lily' adorning the walls. The Jersey Eastern Railway Terminus Hotel Wine Bar, Snow Hill, has existed for many years. It derives its name from the railway station which stood across the road in the cutting beyond the public garden. When it was reconstructed a few years ago new windows were inserted depicting on the glass various scenes relating to the railway of which Major Gilbert More, Kenneth More's father, was the last manager. The Princes, Havre-des-Pas, has been rebuilt in recent years. Its exterior is exactly the same, including the balcony with ornamental iron work, as that of the original public house of years gone by. The Com-

mercial Hotel (originally the Commercial Inn) at the corner of
Conway Street and Commercial Street and the *Soleil Levant*
in Bath Street both have pleasing exteriors. Two of the most
recent additions to the town's many public houses are the Post
Horn (1976), Hue Street, which reproduces the building it
replaced and contains many items connected with the history
of the post office, and No. 10 Wine Bar, which occupies the
first floor and basement of No. 10 Bond Street.

Even before the start of Jersey's tourist industry after 1815,
St Helier had a number of hotels and inns which accommoda-
ted visitors. Among these were the Union Hotel and the York
Hotel, both in the Royal Square, and the British Hotel in
Broad Street. The Union Hotel was demolished when the
present public library was built, but the other two survive
although not as hotels. Once the Napoleonic Wars were over
visitors started coming to the island in ever increasing
numbers and more hotels were opened both in town and
country to cater for their needs. Some of these new hotels had
French proprietors – Hôtel de la Boule d'Or, Grand Hôtel
du Calvados, Grand Hôtel de l'Europe and Hôtel de la
Pomme d'Or (the last two are still in existence). Other hotels
dating from the early years are the Royal Yacht Hotel, Caledonia Place, Star Hotel (now a bank), corner of Mulcaster
Street and Wharf Street, Brée's Royal Hotel (previously
called the Stopford Hotel), David Place, Hôtel de France
(originally the Imperial Hotel) (1866 – by Mr Maberley) near
the town, but actually in St Saviour. A later purpose-built
hotel is the Grand (1890–91 – by T.E. Colcutt), Esplanade.
The Southampton (1899) Weighbridge, has ornamental iron
work. The Palace Hotel, Bagatelle, near the town but actually
in St Saviour, built shortly before World War II, was the
leading hotel of its time. It was destroyed on 7 March 1945
just before the end of the German Occupation.

St Helier has had a regular theatre since 1802. The present
theatre, the Opera House (1900 – by Adolphus Curry)
replaced the Theatre Royal, destroyed by fire in 1899. It was
damaged by fire in 1921 and reconstructed in 1922 by Jesty
and Baker. As it stands to-day the theatre is a pleasant building both outside and inside. Many famous actors, actresses

and entertainers have appeared there including Charles Chaplin and Lillie Langtry, who, incidentally, opened the building. In New Street stands The Playhouse (1937 – reconstruction by C.W. Blanshard Bolton), closed as a theatre some years ago. The town has also had its share of cinemas a number of which have come and gone. The oldest existing cinema, other than the Opera House which was used for some years as such, is The Forum (1935 – by W.F. Hedges), the last building to be constructed of locally produced bricks. During the Occupation the Germans commandeered it for their own use, mainly for the showing of propaganda films or the presentation of stage shows to which the local population was invited but rarely attended. The Odeon Theatre (1952 – by Sir Thomas Bennett), Bath Street, was the first cinema to be built after the war. The most recent cinema is the Ciné de France (1977) which stands in the grounds of the Hôtel de France, St Saviour's Road, St Saviour.

Another place of entertainment is West Park Pavilion (1931 – by Roy C. Blampied) in South African Dutch style.

Victoria College (1850–52 – by John Hayward), Mount Pleasant, St Helier, stands in a commanding position above the east side of the town. The original building is of grey granite and in the Victorian Gothic style. The dressings were of Caen stone but weathered badly and have been largely replaced by granite. The Great Hall which forms part of the building has a fine hammer-beam roof and contains a number of interesting paintings. College House (1899–1901 – by Edmund Berteau), standing across the road from the main college buildings, is constructed of pink granite and roofed with tiles. The New Building (1911 – by Edmund Berteau) is also of granite. The Howard Hall, one of T.B.F. Davis's benefactions, was added in 1934 and has since been converted into a theatre and re-named the Howard Davis Theatre. Nearby is the new octagonal Music School, complete with battlements, which is linked to the theatre by a passage. The college has two libraries, the Dean Jeune Library (for seniors) and the de Quetteville Library (for juniors), as well as fine modern classrooms, including a science block. In the grounds is 'The Temple' (1815 or after: restored 1973), a gazebo in the classical style, consisting of two rooms one above the other and a veranda supported by columns. The top room has a domed ceiling from which is suspended a chandelier. It is used for meetings and receptions: the lower room is used to house the college archives. On the staircase leading to the hall is a memorial (1905) consisting of a brass plate, with granite surround, inscribed with the names of the Old Victorians who fell in the South African War. The World War I memorial takes the form of a bronze statue of Sir Galahad (1924 – by Alfred Turner, A.R.A.) standing on a pedestal of Mont Mado granite in the quadrangle. The inscription is a quotation from Lord Tennyson's *Holy Grail*. The World War II memorial takes the form of an art school (1952 – by Margaret Brodie).

Finally, there is the Masonic Temple (1862–64 – by Thomas Gallichan), Stopford Road, in the neo-classical style and much resembling a Roman temple, and the Victoria Club (1894 – by Adolphus Curry), Beresford Street, in a rather unusual style but for all that looking every inch a club from the days when clubs were clubs.

ST AUBIN, Jersey's second town, stands at the western end of the bay of the same name, where a valley opens to the sea. It emerged into history in the sixteenth century, and from about 1700 to about 1820 it surpassed St Helier as a port, owing to its superior harbour. To-day it is a small and attractive place with an air of prosperity about it. The streets diverge from the vicinity of the harbour and where they climb the surrounding hills they do so steeply, with here and there a tortuous bend.

The earliest plan of St Aubin is probably that reproduced in the Bulletin of La Société Jersiaise for 1897 which shows part of the town as it was in 1775.

As has been stated earlier, the pier was built at the fort between, in, or after 1685 and 1700 attracting many sea captains and merchants to live in St Aubin. The harbour at the town was built between 1754 and 1819.

St Aubin consists of six main thoroughfares: Victoria Road (1844), the name given to the coast road from St Helier as it enters the town, Charing Cross, High Street (La Rue du Croquet), St Aubin's Hill (Mont-les-Vaux) (1865), Market

Hill (La Rue du Moestre), The Bulwarks (Le Boulevard), and Bulwarks Hill (Le Mont du Boulevard), which leads on to Ghost Hill, at the lower end of Mont Arthur.

The steep high street is quaint and attractive, lined as it is with a medley of old houses. On the south side L'Ancienneté (now St Aubyn Hotel) has its roots at least in the eighteenth century and at one time was the home of John Janvrin whose initials appear on the building. Further up the street is Peterborough House, the birthplace of Francis Jeune (1806–68), who became Bishop of Peterborough, hence the name of the house, and further up again is St Magloire, the home of Charles Robin (1743–1824) who founded the firm of Charles Robin & Co. in 1766. On the opposite side is The Hollies bearing the date 1683.

The remains of Le Moulin des Gouttes Pluye (Raindrops Mill) in Mont-les-Vaux are undoubtedly the oldest pieces of masonry in the town. They are all that remain of the mill, mentioned as long ago as 1269, and were purchased by the parish of St Brelade in 1926.

Also in Mont-les-Vaux is the building which until recently housed St Brelade's Hospital (about 1759), a home for old people. At one time the southern part of the premises was the parish hall which accounts for the three detention cells.

On the opposite side of the road is the fine old property La Maison Le Maistre with a marriage stone bearing the initials of John Lemprière and Ann Lemprière (née Durell), his wife, and the date 1706.

There are a number of old houses in The Bulwarks and Bulwarks Hill. Among those worth noting are The Old Court House Hotel which has a fireplace bearing the letters "PƧ" [*sic*] and the date "1611"; La Vieille Maison, built by Peter Le Bailly in 1687, originally with three storeys, later increased to four; La Maison Carteret, dating from at least the early part of the eighteenth century; Rochebois, the original part of which dates from about 1630.

A market existed at St Aubin at least as early as the latter years of the sixteenth century. The premises at present occupied by a bank, although modern, preserve the general form and incorporate the actual granite colonnade and poor-box of the market (1826 – by W. Thompson), which they have replaced.

St Aubin was linked with St Helier by railway in 1870, and the line continued in operation until 1936. The station hotel building (1871) is all that remains of the railway buildings and installations. Since 1948 it has been St Brelade's Parish Hall.

For St Aubin's Methodist Church, St Aubin-on-the-Hill, and the Sacred Heart *see* Chapter 4.

9

The Towns of St Peter Port and St Anne

ST PETER PORT, the capital of Guernsey, stands on the east
coast of the island, and, unlike St Helier, it occupies a hilly
site. On its southern side are fine cliffs stretching for miles
along the coast, and on its northern side is a flattish coastal
area. Looking at the town from the sea there is to be seen the
harbour, on the south side of which stands Castle Cornet
occupying a similar position in relation to the town as does
Elizabeth Castle to St Helier, and on the front the parish
church. Looking from south to north, along the skyline may
be seen the tower of St Barnabas's Church, then the main
building of Elizabeth College, the tower of St James-the-Less
and the Victoria Tower.

The Town, as St Peter Port is familiarly known, is very
ancient, although it is difficult to say with any certainty how
old it is. In 1350 King Edward III ordered that it be enclosed
by a wall, but it is doubtful whether the order was ever carried
out; however, some defence works were built, notably La
Tour Beauregard which stood on the site of St Barnabas's
Church and La Tour Gand which stood at the north end of
the Pollet. Six stones, known as Les Barrières de la Ville,
indicate the limits of the medieval town.

For centuries St Peter Port remained of small extent, but
particularly in the late eighteenth century and early nineteenth century it underwent considerable development.

As in the case of St Helier, it is appropriate to start this
description of St Peter Port at the seat of government, the
Royal Court House which stands in La Rue du Manoir. The
building contains the Court Room, used not only for sittings
of the Royal Court but also for sittings of the States, the
Bailiff's Chambers, the Jurats' Room, the Law Library, the

office of Her Majesty's Greffier and the Public Registry, as well as the Magistrate's Court. It is a dignified granite structure erected between 1792 and 1803. Alterations were effected to the structure in 1822 to the designs of John Wilson, and it was improved in 1899 as a permanent memorial to the Diamond Jubilee of Queen Victoria and considerably enlarged in 1903. The Court House underwent extensive alteration after World War II and was re-opened on 17 June 1949 after many months of work.

At the apex of the front elevation of the building are the arms of the Island and the inscription "G III R 1799"; below and immediately above the main entrance are the Royal Arms.

On the wall of the broad spiral staircase giving access to the upper floor of the Court House are six wooden boards covering a large part of the wall on which are inscribed the names of benefactors and the dates and amounts of their gifts to four charitable funds – the de la Court Fund founded by John de la Court in 1588, the Priaulx Charity Fund founded by John Priaulx in 1837, the Sir William Collings Fund founded in 1849, and the Victoria Fund founded in 1897 to commemorate Queen Victoria's Diamond Jubilee.

In the Court Room the Hanoverian Royal Arms hang above the presidential chair.

In the Jurats' Room two lists hang on the wall, one of all the known bailiffs and the other of all the known jurats.

The prison (1811) stands at the back of the Court House and St James's Chambers (1957 – by J.R. Couchley) containing the offices of the Crown Officers and the police headquarters stands alongside the Court House, which means that someone may be charged, prosecuted, convicted and imprisoned all within a few yards.

Going north from the Royal Court House, past the war memorial, the public garden on the site of St Paul's Methodist Church and the Government office, at the end of Hirzel Street, is Hospital Lane and the Town Hospital, founded in 1741 and opened in 1743. The principal buildings, occupying three sides of a courtyard, have a pleasant aspect. The block facing the entrance archway bears the date 1824. In the board room is a panel on which is a list of the hospital's benefactors since its foundation. The entrance arch, removed from L'Hyvreuse House, bears a panel with the inscription "Hôpital de St. Pierre Port 1742" and another over the arch carved with a pelican in her piety.

Hospital Lane leads on to College Street where is to be found Elizabeth College (1826–29 – by John Wilson), the island's public school for boys, named after Queen Elizabeth I, whose arms appear over the main entrance. The main building, with its square central tower and a square tower at each corner, is in Tudor Gothic style and covered in brown stucco. The school was founded in 1563. The first headmaster was Adrian Saravia (1530–1613), a Fleming, one of the team of translators responsible for the Authorized Version of the Bible.

Grange Road, bordering the south side of the college grounds, is the principal thoroughfare going out of town in a westerly direction and lined on either side with many fine residences. The only one of these properties which will be noticed here is Lukis House with a tower once used as a meteorological station. It is good to know that this interesting building has been preserved and is being put to good use by La Société Guernesiaise (The Guernsey Historical Society). Grange Road leads into Les Gravées, the western limit of the 'New Town'.

College Street, bordering the east side of the college grounds, leads to Candie Road which is bordered on its northern side by the Candie Gardens in which stands the Guernsey Museum and Art Gallery (1978) (on the site of the Candie Gardens Auditorium) with the old bandstand incorporated as a refreshment room. Adjoining the gardens at their western end is the Priaulx Library (formerly Candie House) (about 1780). Close by is Cambridge Park, a delightful open space bordered on its southern side by L'Hyvreuse, a fine row of Georgian and Regency houses, and on its northern side by the Beau Séjour Leisure Centre (1976), which stands on the site of Beau Séjour House. At the west end of L'Hyvreuse is the Duke of Richmond Hotel (1970 – by Lovell and Ozanne) which occupies the site of Grovers Hotel; at the east end is Castle Carey (about 1829 – by John Wilson) with its beautiful garden, and a few yards further on is La Ruette des Côtils (Blue Mountains) where there is a splendid vantage-point for viewing the harbour and the islands beyond.

From the east end of Candie Road it is but a short walk down St Julian's Avenue, passing on the right the Gaumont Cinema (1876 – by William Robilliard) (originally St Julian's Hall and later St Julian's Theatre), to the north end of The Pollet a narrow and partially cobbled thoroughfare, still possessing a certain old-world air. Near the northern end is the Thomas de la Rue, an attractive modern public house with a décor which tells the history of that famous Guernseyman whose name it bears and of the great business which he founded. A bust of de la Rue (1963 – by Eric Peskett) copied from a miniature by L.V. Philips stands in a niche in the corner of the building facing the North Esplanade. On the western side of the street, shortly before reaching Moore's Hotel is one of the old town pumps. Moore's Hotel (about 1760) is a fine grey-granite building, originally the town house of the de Sausmarez family. One of the Barrières de la Ville is situated almost opposite.

The southern end of The Pollet, the east end of Smith Street and the north end of High Street meet at Le Carrefour.

On the north side of Smith Street (La Rue des Forges) is the post office, alongside which is one of Les Barrières de la Ville, and the Philatelic Bureau (opened 1971). On the same side further up the street are Nos. 17, 19 and 21 (about 1840) forming one pleasing architectural group.

High Street (La Grande Rue) is very quaint and attractive. The Town Church presents a pleasing terminal to the south end of the street; the copper dome of the bank at the corner of The Pollet and Smith Street also presents a pleasant terminal at the north end. On the east side nearly opposite the same bank stands the house where Sir Isaac Brock, another famous Guernseyman, lived when he was a child. The ground floor of this once handsome residence is now incorporated into a shop. A plaque affixed to the exterior records Brock's connection with the building.

There are a number of turnings off the High Street meriting investigation. The first (going south) off the western side, through an archway, is Le Fèbvre Street, where the Constables' office occupies a splendid Georgian house (1787), once the property of the Le Marchant family. It is a three-storey building with a fine dressed granite façade with a pedimental porch with Venetian windows above it in the first and second storeys. The second on the same side is Berthelot Street containing two attractive buildings with projecting storeys standing opposite each other. The third, also on the same side, is Commercial Arcade, a pedestrian thoroughfare leading to the markets. The sign above the jeweller's and silversmith's shop at the corner of the High Street and the arcade takes the form of a large Guernsey milkcan. On the east side of the High Street under an archway are the North Pier Steps leading down to the North Pier.

The town has a fine series of markets. The oldest of these are the French Halles (1780–82) with the Old Assembly Rooms above – opened in 1782 – where John Wesley preached in 1787. The latter house the Guille-Allès Library and Museum and are the headquarters of La Société Guernesiaise (founded 1882), entrance being effected through an addition (1886) built in grey granite. Adjoining the west end of the French Halles is the building (1876) formerly housing the Queen's Weights. Opposite are the principal markets, the New Meat Market (1822 – by John Wilson), the Arcades (1830 – by John Wilson), the Fish Market (1875–77 – by John Newton) and the Lower Vegetable Market (1879: original architect John Newton who was replaced by Francis Chambers who completed the project).

In Market Street, a little way from the Guille-Allès Library and on the same side, is the Golden Lion, an old public house with bow windows and a colourful sign.

Continuing westward, Market Street gives way to Mill Street, which in turn gives way to Mansell Street. These two last named thoroughfares are narrow and most attractive. At the western end of Mansell Street is Trinity Square, which in fact is approximately triangular in shape. In the centre of the square is a small garden where there is another of the town pumps, dated 1876, and a horse trough.

Two roads lead back from here into the heart of the town,

Bordage and Pedvin Street. The former merges at its northern end into Fountain Street (about 1830 – by John Wilson), a splendid thoroughfare where is to be found another of Les Barrières de la Ville. Pedvin Street connects with Hauteville a fine street where is to be found Hauteville House (about 1800), the home of Victor Hugo from 1850–70. Hugo purchased the property in 1856, and the city of Paris has owned it since 1927. The property is maintained as it was in the days when it was occupied by Hugo. The interior is remarkable and in every way is indelibly stamped with the strong personality of its famous owner. The building contains a great deal of wood-carving, some of which was done by Hugo himself. The great man's study at the top of the house provides a splendid view of St Peter Port Harbour and beyond.

Down the hill from Hauteville is Cornet Street, a curving thoroughfare of late Georgian and Regency houses which, like Fountain Street, leads to the Town Church (*see* Chapter 2) with the quay and harbour beyond. Just around the corner, on the south side, is the Picquet House (Guardhouse) (1819). Going northwards along the quay the Victoria Pier and the States' Offices (1911) are passed before the weighbridge with its clock tower is reached at the northern end of the North Esplanade, at the landward end of White Rock. A short distance away is the east end of St Julian's Avenue and the Glategny Esplanade. At the corner of the two thoroughfares stands the old established Royal Hotel.

The part of the 'New Town' built atop the cliff, above the 'Old Town' was named Clifton after that district of Bristol, and connected to the 'Old Town' by Constitution Steps, Clifton Steps and Arcade Steps. The development which spread westwards to around Les Gravées, southwards to around Hauteville and Havelet and northwards to around Les Amballes contains streets, terraces and individual houses in the late Georgian, Regency and early Victorian styles. Among streets worth visiting are Allez Street, Doyle Street, George Street, Havilland Street, Little St John Street, Mount Durand, New Street, Queen's Road, St John Street, Sausmarez Street, Union Street, Vauvert and Victoria Road.

Altogether St Peter Port is a delightful town, full of character and interest, occasioned partly by the nature of its site. Streets, lanes and steps ascend and descend at all angles and gradients and at almost every bend and corner, every twist and turn, may be seen some pleasant townscape or seascape. The older parts, such as High Street and The Pollet, narrow and largely granite-paved, are reminiscent of France, while the fine houses and terraces of the 'New Town' recall the elegance of Cheltenham. In addition, St Peter Port presents a fine sight when viewed from offshore – in the foreground Castle Cornet and the harbour and behind the mass of the town with its distinctive skyline which is the hallmark of the place.

ST ANNE, the capital of Alderney, is situated in the western half of the island, more or less equidistant from the north and south coasts. It has a long history, but contains few remains of the past, the majority of its buildings dating from the mid-nineteenth century when the island was enjoying prosperity. Apart from its principal streets it has a number of pleasant little side turnings such as Sauchet Lane.

At the west end of the town is La Triagle, where there is a house with the only doorway with a 'Norman' arch in the island. From there it is but a short distance to Marais Square and Le Huret, the oldest parts of the town, with Royal Connaught Square beyond. In Marais Square is Marais Hotel, old established licensed premises, and the large cattle trough where one waits for the bus.

Royal Connaught Square (originally called St Anne's Square and re-named after the Duke of Connaught's visit in 1905), sports two chestnut trees the smaller of which was planted by Queen Elizabeth II (then Princess Elizabeth) when she visited the island with the Duke of Edinburgh in 1949. On its north side is the former Government House, a dignified granite building standing in pleasant grounds. It was built by John Le Mesurier, the Governor, in 1763 and is now the Island Hall. Also in the square is the Vicarage (1820), and nearby in Les Mouriaux stands Les Mouriaux House, a fine residence built by Peter Le Mesurier in 1779. The ground floor windows of the Vicarage have Victorian gothic glazing bars, a feature to be seen elsewhere in the town.

High Street (La Grande Rue) runs from the east side of the square to the Longis Road. On the north side is the graveyard, clock tower (*see* Chapter 2) and the old school. Above the gateway to the old school is a stone bearing an inscription recording the fact that the school was built and founded by John Le Mesurier, the Governor, in 1790. The building now houses the Alderney Society's excellent museum, opened there in 1972. In this street is the Coronation Inn with a sign depicting the Queen at her coronation and bearing the legend "Duke of Normandy, Queen of Britain". Along the street to the east is the Campania with a stone on which are initials and the date 1743.

Victoria Street (originally called Rue de Grosnez and re-named after Queen Victoria's visit in 1854) is a turning off the north side of High Street and runs northwards. It is the principal thoroughfare of the town. On its west side is St Anne's Church (*see* Chapter 5) and on its east is the Garden of Remembrance (*see* Chapter 11). Opposite the gateway to the churchyard is Ollivier Street which branches off eastwards to Le Val.

Going north up Victoria Street, the first turning on the left is Queen Elizabeth II Street (originally called Rue des Heritiers and later re-named New Street) which, with Victoria Street and Ollivier Street, dates from 1840–60. On the southern side of the street stands the Court House, with the prison at its rear, the whole dating from 1850. The court room (also used for sittings of the States) on the first floor resembled the Royal Court Room in Guernsey, although it was smaller. It was destroyed by the Germans during the Occupation and rebuilt in 1955 more or less as it had existed previously. A plaque affixed to the wall commemorates Captain Herivel, C.B.E., D.S.C., R.N.R., who was President of the States for twenty-one years. On the ground floor are the offices of the Clerk of the Court and the Land Registrar; also the States' Committee Room where hangs a portrait by Opie of Lieutenant-General John Le Mesurier, the last hereditary Governor of Alderney. Over the main entrance of the building are the arms of Alderney.

Around the corner to the west at the north end of Victoria Street is the Methodist Church (1852), successor to a previous church (1813) in Church Street, now the Masonic Temple; around the corner to the east is Les Rocquettes leading to Braye Road which runs to Braye. On the west side of that thoroughfare is the Roman Catholic church of SS Anne and Mary Magdalen (1953–58) replacing the church opened in 1848 and destroyed during the German Occupation. The basement of the present church is used as a social centre. On the east side is Newtown School (1969) where Princess Alexandra unveiled a plaque when she visited the island with her husband, the Hon. Angus Ogilvy, in 1968. Opposite the school to the west, across the road, is an expanse of grass called the Butes with splendid views from its north end across Braye Harbour.

At the end of the road is Braye Street, a row of mid-eighteenth-century houses and warehouses with the pier (1736), part of which is called the Douglas Quay, beyond. John Wesley stayed at what is now the Diver's Inn when he visited the island in 1787.

The narrow granite-paved streets lined as they are with small brightly painted houses, give the town a somewhat French appearance. But, perhaps its most distinctive feature is its dearth of motor traffic resulting in a lack of noise and fumes unusual in this modern world.

10

Buildings of Country and Coast

There are to be found in the country and around the coasts of the principal islands of the Channel Islands a wide variety of buildings, ranging from ancient manor-houses and farmhouses to airport terminal buildings and from windmills to lighthouses.

In Jersey, Guernsey and Sark are a number of manor-houses which are indistinguishable from many other houses. However, a few of them on the three islands are finer both in size and decoration than some others.

Both architecturally and historically St Ouen's Manor, seat of the Malet de Carteret family, situated in the parish of the same name, is the most interesting manor-house in Jersey. The de Carterets had a home in the island, probably the predecessor of the present manor-house, in 1135, and Philip de Carteret obtained permission to crenellate St Ouen's Manor in 1483. The oldest section of this splendid granite-built manor-house is that around and including the tower. The two wings date from the second half of the seventeenth century. The building underwent a major reconstruction and restoration between about 1880 and 1904 under the supervision of Adolphus Curry, the well-known local architect. By the time it was completed the house had something of the appearance of a French château. Entrances to the house include the elegant main doorway on the north-west front, probably late sixteenth century, the small doorway with steps up to it at the angle of the south front, probably dating from the second half of the fifteenth century, and another small doorway with steps up to it on the east front. The heart of the house is the lofty great hall with its splendid staircase. Among the treasures to be seen in the building are family portraits, including those of Sir George Carteret, Bt., and Lady Elizabeth Carteret, his wife, (the latter mentioned in Samuel Pepys's *Diary*) both painted by Sir Peter Lely, and the colourful stained-glass windows by H.T. Bosdet illustrating the history of the de Carteret family and its alliances. There is a buttressed rampart extending along the east terrace and partly on the south-west side of the house and beneath the rampart is the moat. At the northern end of the terrace is a gateway with an arch with two shields, one bearing the arms of Dowse and the other of Poulett: each shield is held by a recumbent lion. The manor has a chapel (*see* Chapter 3) and a dovecot (*see* below). Near the former is a large bowl and pedestal of sandstone. The *tazza*, as it is called, was originally a fountain. The bowl is decorated with four coats of arms – one is that of de Carteret, another is that of Harliston, but two others have not been identified – alternating with grotesque heads through which the water spurted.

In the grounds is a stone to the memory of François Marie Scornet a young Frenchman executed by a German firing squad at the manor on 17 March 1941. Before he was shot he cried out, "*Vive la France!*"

The main entrance to the manor is through a fine granite-built gatehouse with armorial sculpture.

The most spectacular manor-house in Jersey is Trinity, which resembles a French château, a result achieved by an imaginative reconstruction carried out 1910–13 by C. Messervy from designs by Sir Reginald Blomfield, R.A. It has a private chapel. Other manor-houses of interest are: Avranches (present house built 1818), St Lawrence; Diélament, Trinity, with an old granite gateway once the entrance of the original southern avenue; La Hague (rebuilt 1753 and 1871), St Peter; La Haule (1796), St Brelade; La Malletière or La Maison des Prés, Grouville; Les Augrès (probably built about 1800–20), Trinity; Les Colombiers, St Mary; Longueville, St Saviour; Noirmont (present house built 1810), St Brelade; Rozel (built 1770 and enlarged 1820), St Martin; Samarès, with gracious grounds and a canal, St Clement; St Jean La Hougue Boëte (the present house dates from before 1809), St John, with spacious grounds containing a small granite-built chapel (1951) and an ornamental lake;

and Vinchelez de Haut and Vinchelez de Bas, both in St Ouen. Behind the old arch of Vinchelez de Bas Manor on La Route de Vinchelez are parts of the jawbone of a giant whale washed up at Le Pulec, St Ouen, in 1726. Above the keystone of the arch are the arms of de Carteret with the initials "ADC" and the date 1730 with the arms of Dumaresq beneath. La Hague is now a school, La Haule and Longueville are hotels and Les Augrès is now a zoo and the headquarters of the Jersey Wildlife Preservation Trust.

In Guernsey the outstanding manor-house is Sausmarez Manor, St Martin's. The house dates from five different periods and unlike St Ouen's Manor it has not been restored or reconstructed. A small part of what was probably the original manor-house remains which is many centuries old; the second section dates from the sixteenth century; the third is Queen Anne, the fourth is Regency; the fifth is Victorian. The four principal rooms, namely the wainscot room, the drawing-room (1820), the dining-room and the tapestry room are all most pleasing. The Queen Anne house is really beautiful and is built of grey granite with quoins of red granite. It is three-storeyed with a hipped roof and dormers. The roof is surmounted by a gazebo. The front elevation is five windows wide. Raised bands mark the division of the storeys, and the windows are straight-headed. The main entrance giving access to the first floor is by way of a flight of eight steps and a splendid oak door. Inside the house has a fine staircase giving access to the two rooms to be found on each floor. The manor contains a number of interesting paintings, including portraits of Sir Edmund Andros, Captain Philip Saumarez by Sir Henry Wollaston, and Vice-Admiral Philip Durell, who brought Philip Saumarez's body home after he had been killed in action. This latter portrait shows the Admiral holding a scroll inscribed "A Plan of Louisburg 1745", for the capture of which Canadian town he was largely responsible. Portraits of four generations of the de Sausmarez family hang above the beautiful sideboard in the dining-room. In the same room is a painting, by the celebrated Jersey marine artist Peter Monamy (c. 1670–1749), showing the capture of the French ship of the line, *Mars*, by H.M.S. *Nottingham* commanded by Philip Saumarez. On the other side of the chimney-breast is another marine picture, this time by Thomas Whitcombe. Silhouettes of some of Thomas de Sausmarez's twenty-eight children are to be seen on the wall of the staircase in the Queen Anne part of the house. Among the many other treasures to be seen are the wedding coat of King James II, the diary of Sir Edward de Carteret (*c*. 1630–98), Bailiff of Jersey; and the log book of H.M.S. *Centurion* (published 1974) kept by Philip Saumarez when he was the ship's first lieutenant on her famous voyage around the world. In front of the house is a croquet lawn and flower beds, and beyond, bordering the road, are white painted railings and gates. The gate pillars are surmounted by the supporters of the de Sausmarez arms, a unicorn and a greyhound, each holding a shield; the outer pillars bear the family's arms (a falcon displayed). All the carving was executed by Sir Henry Cheere, a leading sculptor of the eighteenth century. Close by this entrance to the manor grounds stands the court house of the Fief Sausmarez. The court room on the ground floor is older than the upper floor, which was added in the eighteenth century. In the first floor room there is a fireplace surrounded by blue and white Delft tiles representing biblical scenes.

Other interesting manor-houses in Guernsey are Anneville with a chapel and a court house, Les Câches, Les Eperons and Les Granges (1685). The last mentioned is a fine granite-built house (the third known to have been built on the site) with an arched doorway, a *bénitier* (*see* p.166), a huge granite fireplace downstairs and other granite fireplaces upstairs. The original gateway to the manor grounds, now occupied by other properties, is known as Ivy Gates, and comprises a large arch for wheeled traffic and a small arch for pedestrians; the keystone of the larger arch bears the de Beauvoir Arms. The gateway, which dates from about 1740, was restored in 1968.

The only manor-house in Sark is La Seigneurie, the home of the Lord of Sark. It is not the original manor-house built by Helier de Carteret in 1565, and only became known as La Seigneurie after Suzanne Le Pelley became Lady of Sark by purchasing the Lordship in 1730. Like the first manor-house, it was originally built in 1565 and was known as La Perron-erie. It was probably rebuilt by Jean Le Gros in 1675, the date appearing over the fireplace in the hall; the sundial on the south-west corner of the house is dated 1685 and bears his initials. The windows on the ground-floor front were enlarged in 1732 with granite brought from Jersey, and in the same year chestnut panelling was installed in some of the bedrooms. In 1854 a new wing was added, as well as the tower, used for signalling to Guernsey, which is rather out of keeping with the rest of the building. Many of the old records of the island are preserved at La Seigneurie. Adjacent to the house are two buildings with an ecclesiastical appearance. Nothing much is known about them and it is doubtful whether they are of any historical interest. The manor-house has a beautiful walled garden. The fine wrought-iron gates (1929) at the entrance to La Seigneurie were a gift by the islanders to the Dame of Sark on her marriage to Robert W. Hathaway. In the grounds is preserved a brass cannon bearing the inscription: "*Don de Sa Majesté la Royne Elizabeth au Seigneur de Sercq A.D. 1572*"; the mounting dates from 1968.

The manor-house on Herm is not a manor-house in the true sense. However, it is the residence of the Tenant of the island. It is a large crenellated house standing in the centre of the island. It was described by Sir Compton Mackenzie, Tenant from 1920 to 1923, as "externally perhaps the ugliest building in Europe". Not far from the manor-house is a round tower with a crenellated parapet.

From early times it was the privilege of the lord of the manor to have a dovecot in which to keep his pigeons. Later the privilege was extended, and certain people who were not lords of the manor were allowed to have pigeon-holes inserted in their houses. Jersey has eleven dovecots which are to be found at the following manors: St Ouen (modern), Rozel (conical roof), Samarès, Trinity (modern reconstruction), La Hague (restored), Longueville (rebuilt 1692 and now the property of The National Trust for Jersey), Le Colombier (1669), Les Colombiers (restored), Diélament (rebuilt 1573) which is the largest and has 1,450 nest holes, La Haule (square) and Hamptonne or La Patente (square, dated 1674).

Hamptonne and Le Colombier are not generally regarded as manors, although the former was raised to manorial status by King Charles II in 1649. The de Carteret-Dumaresq Arms were not inserted into the exterior of the dovecot at La Hague until 1879. Guernsey has one dovecot situated at Torteval which belonged to the Fief au Cannely, and was restored some years ago. In Sark a picturesque dovecot (1730) stands at the back of La Seigneurie.

Jersey, Guernsey and Sark possess a great many attractive old farmhouses, some of which are substantial structures. They are all built of stone to a more or less standard plan. The vast majority of these old houses consist of a ground floor and first floor; the old Guernsey and Sark houses had only a ground floor. In the older two-storeyed houses in Guernsey the front door has two windows on one side and one on the other, and there are four windows on the first-floor frontage. In Jersey and in the later Guernsey houses the front door is in the centre and has two windows on either side; there are five windows on the first-floor frontage, one above each of the ground-floor windows and one above the front door. The vast majority of the windows are of the sash variety, although originally the older houses had smaller windows of a different type. In the older ones the front door opening has a curved lintel instead of a straight one. In Guernsey, in addition to the stones forming the arch, there is a second row immediately above them which is as large as the first. A Jersey and Guernsey custom, almost certainly not older than the eighteenth century, was for the lintel of the front door to be carved with the initials of the husband and wife and the date of their marriage; sometimes intertwined hearts were also included. There is at least one example of a marriage stone recording two generations of marriages. Modern examples of marriage stones are occasionally seen. Mrs Joan Stevens in her book *Old Jersey Houses Volume II* lists no less than 903 of these stones. Originally these farmhouses were thatched, but nowadays they are all either tiled or slated. The stones which protrude from the large chimney-stacks of many of these old dwellings date from when the roofs were of thatch and were designed to prevent water seeping underneath it. These stones, as well as the ends of fireplace corbels protruding through a gable wall, are called 'witches' stones'. It is said that their object was to provide resting places for witches so as to prevent them from going down the chimney to rest inside the house. Some houses still possess a circular stone staircase contained in a tower called a *tourelle*. Inside the older farmhouses are found huge fireplaces, either with wooden or granite lintels.

In the Jersey Museum are reproductions of a traditional kitchen and bedroom, containing many structural features removed from old farmhouses, as well as original furniture and household utensils. A similar display may be seen at the Folk Museum in Saumarez Park, Guernsey.

In a number of Jersey houses and in a few in Guernsey are found niches called *bénitiers*, often adjacent to the front door or at the foot of the stairs. They have an ecclesiastical appearance, and if they were to be found in churches or chapels would be designated either piscinae or holy water stoups, each according to its particular characteristics. Some people say that they were removed from churches and chapels at the time of the Reformation; others, that similar features may be found in old houses in Normandy and Brittany and there they are of secular origin and for domestic use. The number of these niches in private dwellings in Jersey would lead one to believe that some, at least, are of secular origin. In Guernsey there are not so many *bénitiers* – the finest is said to be that at Les Grands Moulins at Castel, others are at Les Effards in the same parish, at La Maison du Haut, St Peter's, and Les Granges Manor, St Peter Port.

At the end of some farmhouses is a small dower-house representing 'the widow's third', that is a widow's entitlement to the life enjoyment of one-third of her late husband's real estate.

Many of the farmhouses have extensive outbuildings; formerly in Jersey these invariably included pigsties and a press-house. In the latter were located a circular granite cider trough with a large granite wheel for crushing the apples into pulp and a press for extracting the juice from the pulp.

At the entrance to a number of old Jersey farms are two

round-headed archways, the larger for vehicles and the smaller for pedestrians. Similar double archways occur in Guernsey.

In Guernsey there are a number of splendidly carved doors, the work of John Burgess (1818–1904), wood-carver and cabinet-maker. A splendid example of such a door is to be seen at La Pompe, La Contrée de Mouilpieds, St Martin's.

The National Trust for Jersey is fortunate in owning three traditional Jersey farmhouses, Morel Farm, St Lawrence, La Valette, St John, and The Elms, St Mary, as well as Le Rât Cottage, St Lawrence, probably dating from the late seventeenth century. The National Trust of Guernsey owns an old Guernsey cottage in the Talbot Valley.

In addition to the manor-houses and farmhouses there are scattered throughout Jersey and Guernsey a large number of interesting houses of varying styles and ages. Of these, the most spectacular is undoubtedly La Haye du Puits, Castel, Guernsey, with its attractive turrets. Another fine property in the same island and parish is Saumarez Park, an eighteenth-century house belonging to the States and now housing the Hostel of St John, which is a home for elderly men and women; the spacious grounds, partly laid out as a formal garden, are used for agricultural and horticultural shows.

In years gone by there were in both Jersey and Guernsey many watermills of which only a limited number remain. Alderney has a watermill which stands at the bottom of Val de la Bonne Terre, between Fort Tourgis and Platte Saline, and belongs to the Alderney Society which has carried out restoration work on the building. The National Trust for Jersey has fully restored Quetivel Mill in St Peter's Valley and won a well merited Civic Trust Award for its work. Les Niots Mill, Les Niaux, Talbot Valley, Castel, Guernsey, also has been restored recently.

Jersey has four windmills – Grouville, Rozel, St Ouen (possibly early nineteenth century but which occupies a site where a windmill has stood for 400 or even 600 years) and St Peter (1837). Grouville, Rozel and St Ouen are used as sea marks, and the latter is the headquarters of the 18th (St Ouen's) Scout Group. There has been a windmill at Grouville at least as early as 1331 and one at Rozel at least as early as 1219. St Peter's is now part of a public house and restaurant and sports a new set of sails.

Guernsey has five windmills – Le Hêchet or Ozanne's Mill (1825), Ruette Braye, and Sausmarez Mill, both in St Martin's; Les Vardes, St Peter Port, and Mont Saint, now converted into a dwelling house with castellations, St Saviour's, both cement mills dating from the nineteenth century; Vale Mill, increased to almost double its original height by the Germans during the Occupation, in the parish of the same name.

Sark has two windmills, one on Great Sark built by Helier de Carteret in 1571 and another on Little Sark which was built later. The former standing on the highest point of the island, 375 feet above sea level, without its sails but with all its internal machinery, including the millstones, belongs to the Lord of Sark. The de Carteret Arms are carved on the lintel of the door and the weathervane bears the date 1571.

Not surprisingly, there are a number of lighthouses around the coasts of the Channel Islands. The best known is probably that on Les Casquets, a dangerous reef of rocks about a half a mile across. The northern rock is conical in shape and on it stands the lighthouse. Originally there were three lighthouses – St Peter, St Thomas and the Donjon, but when Trinity House assumed responsibility for them in 1877 the two latter were abolished and the third improved. Corbière Lighthouse, St Brelade, Jersey, is interesting as an early example of a concrete structure. It was designed by Sir John Coode and completed in November 1873, the light being lit experimentally for the first time on 24 April of the following year. At the side of the slipway leading to the lighthouse is a tablet recording how in 1946 Peter Larbalestier gave his life in attempting to rescue a visitor cut off by the incoming tide. Les Hanois Lighthouse stands on Le Biseau Rock a mile and a quarter out to sea off the south-west tip of Guernsey. It is built of Cornish granite and rises 117 feet above its base; it was first lit officially on 8 December 1862. An attractive lighthouse (1866 – by Peter Le Lièvre) stands at the end of the breakwater at the entrance to St Peter Port Harbour. Mannez Lighthouse in

Alderney rises to a height of 120 feet and dates from 1912. Sark's lighthouse, which also dates from 1912, is located at the end of a long flight of steps at Point Robert and may be seen from the sea just before entering Maseline Harbour.

Five unusual buildings are: the small granite structure on the Trinity Main Road astride the boundary of St Helier and Trinity, Jersey, erected in order to give the owner the right to vote in both parishes; the bridge (by W. Quitter) with fine granite towers built across La Route de Carteret, Castel, Guernsey, by the fourth Lord de Saumarez to enable him to walk from Saumarez Park to the sea without leaving his own property; the tiny barrel-roofed Sark Prison (1856) with its two cells; the circular nineteenth-century Herm Prison or Lock-Up standing close to the tennis court of the White House Hotel; the oxen-shoeing stance, with a tiled (formerly thatched) roof, near the farm buildings in Herm.

11

Statues and Memorials

There are five statues of royalty in the Channel Islands. The oldest is that of King George II (1751 – by John Cheere) which stands on a fine granite plinth (1819), with the King's monogram surmounted by a crown, carved on its western face, at the eastern end of the Royal Square, St Helier, on or near the site of the market cross destroyed at the Reformation. The statue, made of lead and gilded, depicts the King in the garb of a Roman Emperor. All distances in the island are measured from the base of the statue and laws are promulgated by the Viscount (Sheriff) from a stone at the foot of the western face of the plinth. Proclamations of Accession are read from a platform erected in front of the statue. The Prince Consort is commemorated by a bronze statue (1863 – by Joseph Durham) which stands at the top of the Albert Pier, St Peter Port. A medal was struck to commemorate the unveiling of the statue. It is 1½ inches in diameter, ⅛ inch thick and has raised edges. The obverse shows the statue with the name "GUERNSEY" beneath it; the reverse shows a laurel wreath within which is the legend "In Remembrance of ALBERT the GOOD, 1863". The only known example of the medal is in the Guille-Allès Museum. Jersey and Guernsey each possess a statue of Queen Victoria. That in the former island (1890 – by Georges Wallet) was originally set up in the centre of the Weighbridge Gardens, St Helier, and when these were removed to make way for a bus depot it was re-erected in the centre of the car park at the top of the harbour. In 1976 it was transferred to a site at the southern end of the Triangle Park at West Park. The statue stands 7 feet high on a plinth of La Moye granite designed by Adolphus Curry. The front of the plinth is carved with the Queen's monogram surmounted by a crown and at the base is the inscription *"Erigé par le peuple"* (Erected by the people); its two sides bear the dates 1837 and 1887. That in the latter island (1900 – by C.B. Birch) is a replica of the original erected in Bombay and stands at the top end of the Candie Gardens. A statue of King George V (1939 – by Sir William Reid Dick) stands on a granite plinth a short distance inside the main entrance of the Howard Davis Park, St Helier. On the front of the plinth is carved a crown above the inscription "H.M. KING GEORGE V 1865–1936".

The Victoria Tower (1848 – by William Bunn Collings), Monument Road, St Peter Port, was built to commemorate the visit of Queen Victoria and Prince Albert to the island in 1846. It is 96 feet high and stands on the site of Le Moulin de l'Hyvreuse. It is a heavily crenellated square tower surmounted by an octagonal tower of red Cobo granite.

At the eastern end of the Lower Park, on the north side of Victoria Avenue, St Helier, is a granite monument which takes the form of a pedestal surmounted by a crown on a cushion and commemorates Queen Victoria's Diamond Jubilee. On the south side of the pedestal is the inscription "Victoria Avenue 22nd June, 1897".

Lieutenant-General Sir George Don, Lieutenant-Governor of Jersey (1806–14), who previously had commanded in Jersey as Lieutenant-Colonel of the 59th Regiment, is commemorated by a monument (1885 – by Pierre Robinet) in The Parade, St Helier, which takes the form of a group of three statues of cast iron or an alloy on a platform of Mont Mado granite approached by steps and flanked by old cannons. Don stands on a plinth at the centre with the seated figure of Commerce on one side and of Industry on the other. On the east face of the plinth bearing Don's statue is the inscription *"A Don 1806 à 1814"*.

Lieutenant-General Sir John Doyle, Lieutenant-Governor of Guernsey (1803–15), is commemorated by a memorial taking the form of a granite column standing on the summit of the little hill at Jerbourg, St Martin's, Guernsey. On its base is the following inscription:

This Monument was erected by the States of Guernsey in 1953 in memory of Sir John Doyle, K.C.B., Lieutenant-Governor of Guernsey 1803–1815. It replaces the original Monument which was erected in 1825 and destroyed by the Germans in 1944 during the occupation of the Island.

Sir Winston Churchill is commemorated by the memorial park bearing his name at St Brelade's Bay, Jersey, where there is a rough-hewn block of grey granite from L'Etacq Quarries bearing a bronze relief portrait of Sir Winston's head and shoulders and the inscription "The Rt. Hon. Sir Winston Leonard Spencer Churchill, K.G., O.M., C.H. 'And our dear Channel Islands are also to be free today' 8th May, 1945".

St Sampson's Harbour has two large monuments. The first (erected 1873), standing at the south-west corner of the Crocq, takes the form of a stone 13 feet high, formerly part of a dolmen, with an inscription on its southern face paying tribute to Daniel de Lisle Brock, Bailiff of Guernsey (1821–42), under whose presidency the States voted the first works for the improvement of the harbour. The second is an obelisk 27 feet high (erected about 1873 – by James Duquemin), surmounted by a light, standing at the eastern end of the Crocq. It is of blue-grey granite with an inscription on its western face, on a raised polished panel, to the States' Committee concerned with improvements to the harbour, and another inscription on its eastern face as follows "1873. Messire P. Stafford Carey, Bailiff".

Daniel de Lisle Brock is again commemorated by a bust which graces the front of the premises of a bank on the east side of the High Street, St Peter Port.

Three Jersey constables (each Jersey parish has a constable who not only is equivalent to a mayor but also has police powers and is a member of the States) are commemorated by public memorials: Peter Le Sueur and Philip Baudains, both constables of St Helier, the former from 1839–53 and the latter from 1881–96, and Philip Le Vesconte, constable of Trinity, 1868–77 and 1890–1909. Both Le Sueur and Baudains were advocates and, in addition, Le Sueur was from 1846 the treasurer of the States.

Le Sueur's memorial takes the form of an obelisk (1855–56

– by A. Gallichan) on the island at the eastern end of Broad Street, St Helier, facing the building which replaced the house where he was born. The work of building the memorial was carried out by Thomas and John Le Cras. In *The Gossiping Guide to Jersey* (1863) J.B.P. Payne, the author, expressed his dislike of the memorial thus:

> The monument itself is a sad blot on the good taste of the island, and is merely an exaggeration of those spa toys one buys at Sandown or Clifton. At each side of its square base, are lions' heads, pierced for fountains. The water however has never been forthcoming, so the lions look like hapless sea-voyagers – retching without effect. We do not know who designed this thing – this cross between a pillar and a post. We wish we did, for his name ought to go down to posterity, encircled with the halo that should belong to the inventor of the ugliest bit of pillo-pyramidical construction in the world.

The four sides of the base of the obelisk are inscribed as follows: west, *"A Pierre Le Sueur ses Concitoyens Reconnaissants"*; north, *"Cinq fois élu Connétable de St. Hélier"*; east (on a bronze plaque), "This Monument was erected by his grateful fellow Citizens to Peter Le Sueur, Born Nov. 20th 1811: Died Jan. 16th 1853"; south, *"Il se dévoua au bien-être de son pays"*.

At each corner of the surround is a cast-iron gas lamp-standard, now converted to electricity.

In Green Street Cemetery is the private memorial to Le Sueur which takes the form of another obelisk, with an urn at its apex. There are inscriptions on three sides at the base. The one on the south side relates to Le Sueur and those on the other sides are to members of his family.

Baudains' memorial (1897 – by Adolphus Curry) takes the form of a bust of the constable on a granite pedestal surrounded by iron railings with the monogram "P.B." worked into their design. There are inscriptions on the four sides of the pedestal as follows: west, "Philip Baudains, Mayor of St. Helier, 1881–1896"; north, *"Erigé par souscription publique en reconnaissance de services rendus à son pays, 1897"*; east, *"Philippe Baudains, 15 années Connétable de St. Hélier, 1881–1896"*; south, "Erected by public subscription in recognition of services rendered to his country, 1897". The sculptor was A. McFarlane Shannan of Glasgow, the granite work was executed by F.T. Carter and the railings were made by H. Webber. The granite came from Ronez, St John. The memorial, which stands in the western section of the Parade Gardens, St Helier, was subscribed for by 1,000 people who donated £330.

Le Vesconte's memorial (1910) stands at Les Croix, Trinity. It takes the form of a granite obelisk with suitable surround.

Possibly the only centenier (each Jersey parish has a number of centeniers who are honorary policemen) to be killed in the course of his duties was Centenier George Le Cronier. On 28 February 1846, accompanied by constable's officer Henry Luce Manuel, he called at Mulberry Cottage, Patriotic Street, St Helier, to arrest Marie Le Gendre and her husband on the charge of keeping a house of ill repute. Her husband was out and when the centenier attempted to take her into custody Marie Le Gendre snatched up a carving knife and plunged it into his stomach. *"Oh, mon garçon, je suis stabbé,"* exclaimed the stricken centenier as he clutched his stomach and lurched into the street. The constable's officer avoided Marie Le Gendre's second lunge and rushed out of the house shouting "Murder! Murder!" and looking for help. Le Cronier died the following day. In the criminal proceedings which followed Marie Le Gendre was found guilty of 'voluntary homicide' and banished from Jersey for life. The obituary notice on Le Cronier published in *La Chronique de Jersey* rather surprisingly stated that "One might say of him that he hadn't an enemy". After the death of her husband Marie Le Gendre married again. By a strange coincidence her second husband's name was Le Cronier.

A huge granite memorial (1848–49 – by J. Hayward and modified by T. Gallichan) 25 feet high, was erected to the memory of Centenier Le Cronier at the southern end of Green Street Cemetery, St Helier. The memorial takes the form of a rectangular base on which is an urn surmounted by a canopy supported by four columns, bearing an inscription in French which reads in English as follows: "This honourable citizen, at a time when he was carrying out the duties of his office, received from a guilty hand, a fatal wound. His fellow citizens, wishing to perpetuate their regrets and the memory of his devotion, have erected this monument over his mortal remains". Other members of the family, including the centenier's widow, are commemorated on a stone at the foot of the memorial.

Down the centuries Channel Islanders have been staunch in their loyalty to England (later Great Britain). They served in the local militias and guarded their native islands against attack by the enemy; they also served (a number still do) in the regular forces of the Crown and had a splendid record of service in both World Wars. Therefore, it is not surprising that throughout the islands may be seen insular, parochial, institutional and private memorials to those who have died for King and Country.

The Battle of Jersey, 6 January 1781, is recorded by a stone let into the paving of the Royal Square, St Helier.

The South African War Memorial (by W. Newbury), St Julian's Avenue, St Peter Port, erected to the memory of the officers and men of Guernsey and Alderney who died in the South African War 1891–1902, was unveiled by the Duke of Connaught in 1905.

Jersey's war memorial, the Cenotaph (1923 – by Charles de Gruchy), is located at the eastern end of the Parade Gardens, St Helier. It is built of grey granite from La Moye and enclosed by low ornamental railings. The pedestal with the pylon supports a sarcophagus containing a roll of honour. The inscription on the south side reads: "OUR GLORIOUS DEAD – THEIR NAME LIVETH FOR EVER MORE", that on the north side reads: "JERSEY A SES ENFANTS MORTS POUR LA PATRIE" (Jersey to her children who died for their country), on the east and west sides are the dates "1914–1918" and "1939–1945". Guernsey's war memorial (1926) is at the top of Smith Street, St Peter Port; Alderney's stands in the Garden of Remembrance in Victoria Street, St Anne, and Sark's stands in front of St Peter's Church.

The Military Cemetery, Fort George, St Peter Port, contains the graves of British and German soldiers. It was the garrison cemetery and contains a memorial to members of the British forces who died during World War I and are buried in this and other churchyards and cemeteries in Guernsey, Alderney and Sark. On the gateway is an inscription in English and German to one hundred and eleven German soldiers of World War II who are buried in the cemetery.

Jack Counter Memorial, Jack Counter Close, First Tower, St Helier, perpetuates the memory of Jack Counter who when serving as a private in World War I was awarded the Victoria Cross for carrying a message in the face of fierce fire at Boisleaux St Mare in 1918 after several of his comrades had died in the attempt.

The S.S. *Vega*, the Red Cross ship which brought supplies to the Channel Islands towards the end of the German Occupation is commemorated by granite stones spelling out 'V E G A 1945' set into the paving of the Royal Square, St Helier.

Island War Cemetery (1943), Howard Davis Park, Route du Fort, St Saviour. Fifty-one burials of British and Allied servicemen (including one exhumation from St Brelade's Churchyard) were made in the cemetery between 6 June 1943 and 1 December 1944. In June 1946 the bodies of the American servicemen were exhumed, handed over to the United States authorities and removed from Jersey. Each grave is marked by an oak cross with the name and rank (where known) and date of burial of the deceased. The cemetery is beautifully maintained and flowers are grown on each grave.

The Free French Memorial (1963), Parade, St Helier, which stands close to Elizabeth Place, was erected by L'Association des Français Libres to thank the people of Jersey for the help afforded to Frenchmen on the way to the United Kingdom in response to the appeal of 18 June 1940.

Slave workers' memorials are to be seen in Jersey and in Alderney. In the former island the memorial is to be seen in the grounds of the crematorium at Westmount and is to the memory of French, Spanish and Russians who died in the island during the German Occupation. In the latter island, where the road to Saye Bay joins the main coast road, there is a memorial (1967 – by A.R. Warren) established through the generosity and interest of the Hammond family to the slave workers of all nations who died in the island during World War II.

At White Rock, St Peter Port Harbour, let into the wall is a stone with an inscription recording the names of members of the civilian population who lost their lives as the result of an enemy air raid that took place on 28 June 1940; it is also a memorial to all Guernsey people who died as the result of hostilities 1939–45.

Not surprisingly, the islands contain a number of monuments to those who have been drowned around their treacherous shores.

The Pilcher Memorial takes the form of a granite obelisk situated on the cliff above Havre Gosselin, Sark. It was raised:

IN MEMORY OF

Jeremiah Giles Pilcher, Esq., J.P., D.L., Merchant of London; Agnew Giffard, Esq., C.E., Walter J. Giffard, Esq., his brother; Dr. C.S. Gatehouse; and Mansell Renouf, Boatman; who embarked in a sailing-gig from the bay below this spot at 5 p.m. on the 19th October, 1868, and were all lost during a squall of wind which soon afterwards arose with heavy wind and thick darkness, etc.

The Harvey Memorial (1871), at the foot of Mount Bingham, St Helier, taking the form of a granite obelisk, with inscription, was erected by the Foresters of Jersey to the memory of Captain Henry Beckford Harvey and the gallant crew of the steamer *Normandy* which collided in a dense fog with another vessel, the *Mary*, thirteen miles off the Needles on 17 March 1870 and was so damaged that she rapidly sank. The boats were lowered, and every passenger was placed in them, but there was no room for the captain and fourteen other members of the ship's company, who calmly sacrificed their lives to save those committed to their care. Sixteen passengers were drowned; eighteen passengers and twelve members of the crew were saved. The obelisk was removed to its present site in 1873.

The Westaway Memorial (1875 – by Pierre Robinet) standing beside the Harvey Memorial commemorates the gallantry

of John H. Westaway, a passenger who displayed great cool-
ness and courage when the *Normandy* sank. It was removed to
its present site in 1888. The memorial takes the form of a
fountain composed of a serpent wound round an anchor, in
the centre of a large shallow bowl standing on a plinth, around
which is a low surround. Let into the plinth is a relief portrait
of Westaway with an inscription beneath. The area between
the plinth and the surround is planted with flowers. At the
base of the anchor appear the words "By Grandin, founders,
Jersey".

A commemorative plaque to Henry W. Kinloch, another
passenger who displayed great courage on the same occasion,
was erected at the Royal Military College, Sandhurst.

The Prosperity Memorial (1975), L'Erée, Guernsey, commemorates one of Guernsey's worst shipwrecks, the loss of
the *Prosperity* off the west coast during a storm in 1974. All
the crew perished and when their bodies were recovered they
were buried at Foulon Cemetery, St Peter Port. The ship was
carrying a cargo of timber and after the shipwreck quantities
of timber were washed ashore.

The Gorey shipbuilders are commemorated by a granite
skeletal boat (1978 – by C.P. Warren) which stands in the
gardens on the front at Gorey, St Martin, Jersey.

The Vardon Memorial (1966), Grouville Golf Links,
Jersey, is a simple stone beside the thirteenth fairway to the
memory of Henry William (Harry) Vardon (1870–1937), the
famous Jersey-born golfer who was six times open champion –
1896, 1898, 1899, 1903, 1911 and 1914. The inscription
declares that Vardon was born "Within putting distance of
this stone".

The Luscombe Plaque, St Catherine's Breakwater, St
Martin, Jersey, commemorates the feat of Miss Jane
Luscombe, aged fifteen years, in swimming around the island
on 5 August 1976. She departed from St Catherine's at 4.35
a.m. and arrived back at 5.40 p.m.

Victor Hugo (1952), Rocher des Proscrits, to the west of
the slipway at Le Dicq, St Helier, was inserted by La
Société Jersiaise on 23 June commemorates Victor Hugo's
exile in Jersey 1852–5. His statue (1914 – by J. Boucher) in

the Candie Gardens, St Peter Port, is, without doubt, the most striking statue in the Channel Islands, depicting the poet in thoughtful mood, looking downwards with his right hand to his beard. His legs are wide apart, his outer garments and scarf are caught by the breeze and he is holding his hat and his stick in his left hand. The statue is full of movement and it appears that at any moment Hugo will leave his rocky pedestal and go striding down the lawn on his way to Hauteville House. The statue bears his name, his dates (1802–85) and his tribute to the people of the Channel Islands.

The Le Beir Monument, taking the form of a grey-granite, 20 feet high (including the mound) obelisk stands at the centre of the Fairfield near Castel Church, Guernsey. It was erected by the Royal Guernsey Agricultural Society in 1860 to the memory of Nicholas Le Beir, secretary of the society 1842–57.

The Walter Memorial takes the form of a grey stone on which are a cross and the inscription "E.C.L.W. 4th May, 1885" let into the bank of the Longy Road, Alderney, not far from the ninth green of the golf course. It is to the memory of Captain Edward Charles Lethridge Walter of the 83rd, County of Dublin, Regiment, who was killed on the road while driving his horse-drawn tandem.

The Herm Obelisk (1835), variously known as La Pierre aux Rats, Mansell's Monument and The Mark of the Rock Caval, stands at the north end of the Sandy Plain close to Maussonnière beach and occupies the site of La Longue Pierre or La Pierre aux Rats. It is stone-built, 25 feet high and has a square base in which is a recess. La Longue Pierre had served as a sea-mark and when it was demolished by the Herm Granite Company the local fishermen complained so strongly that the company was compelled to build the obelisk as a replacement.

Green Street Cemetery (1827), Green Street, St Helier, Jersey, contains a number of noteworthy memorials: George Le Cronier (died 1846) and Peter Le Sueur (died 1853) (*see* above); Pierre Emilie Langelier (died 1857) whose murder resulted in the trial of Madelaine Smith, a famous case in Scottish legal history – inscription only, the body is buried elsewhere; Zéno Boleslas Swietoslawski (died 1875) a native of Warsaw and a famous Polish patriot.

Macpela Cemetery (1851), St John, Jersey. Following Louis Napoleon's *coup* in 1851 some two hundred political refugees went to live in Jersey. Two years later it was estimated that there were two hundred and twenty-six of these exiles on the island, including one hundred and eight French, ten Italian and eight German and Hungarian. Among them were a number of colourful figures of whom Victor Hugo was pre-eminent. Some of the political refugees died in exile and were buried in a communal grave. Each burial was made the occasion for a funeral oration extolling liberty and freedom and condemning oppressors. Several of these orations were delivered by Hugo. Standing on the grave is a pillar on which there are a number of oval copper discs each inscribed with the name of one of the exiles buried there, as well as three gravestones each commemorating one deceased. Long after the grave was full and the exiles had left the island one of their number who had settled there died and he had to be buried in another grave where a small granite stone with a copper disc was erected to his memory. Another exile, Paul Harro-Harring (1798–1870), a Dane, is also buried in the cemetery and commemorated by a stone.

The only other cemeteries to be noticed here are: The General or Almorah Cemetery (1855: chapel and lodges 1858 – by Poulton and Woodman), Richmond Road, St Helier, and the Animals' Cemetery (1928), First Tower, St Helier; Candie Cemetery (1831), Upland Road, St Peter Port; Foulon Cemetery (1856: chapel (now a crematorium), lodge and gateway – by Poulton and Woodman), Route Isabelle, St Peter Port.

Select Bibliography

ASQB, *Alderney Society and Museum Quarterly Bulletin*
BSJ, *Société Jersiaise Annual Bulletin*
RGS, *The Review of the Guernsey Society*
TSG, *Report and Transactions of La Société Guernesiaise*

AHIER, P., *The Governorship of Sir Walter Ralegh in Jersey 1600–1603*, Bigwood Printers Ltd. (Jersey, 1971)
—, *Stories of Jersey Seas of Jersey's Coast and of Jersey Seamen*, The Advertiser Press Ltd. (Huddersfield, Part I 1955, Part II 1956 and Part III 1957)
ANONYMOUS, *A Brief History of the Parish Church of Holy Trinity*, (Jersey, n.d.)
—, *Saint Peter's Church*, (Jersey, n.d.)
—, *St Clement's, Jersey – The Church and Parish*, (Jersey, n.d.)
—, *St John-in-the-Oak-Wood, Jersey – A Brief History of the Church*, (Jersey, 1976)
—, *St Matthew's Church*, (Jersey, n.d.)
—, *The Parish Church of St Martin de Grouville*, (Jersey, n.d.)
—, *The Story of St Sampson's Church Guernsey*, (Gloucester, n.d.)
—, [Oldfield] *Some Account of Mont Orgueil Castle in the Island of Jersey*, P. Payn (Jersey, 1838)
BALLEINE, G.R., *A Biographical Dictionary of Jersey*, Staples Press (London, 1948)
BELLIS, R., *Peintures Murales dans L'Eglise de St Clément*, BSJ 1880 (Jersey, 1880)
BOIS, F. DE L., *The Parish Church of St Saviour, Jersey*, Phillimore (London & Chichester, 1976)
BRETT, C.E.B., *Buildings in the Town and Parish of St Peter Port*, (National Trust of Guernsey, 1975)
—, *Buildings of the Island of Alderney*, (The Alderney Society, 1976)
—, *Buildings in the Town and Parish of Saint Helier*, (The National Trust for Jersey, 1977)
BRYANS, P., *A Guide to Batterie Lothringen Noirmont Point*,

Channel Islands Occupation Society (Jersey Branch) (Jersey, 1978)

CACHEMAILLE, J.L.V., *The Island of Sark*, A.G. Reynolds & Co. Ltd. (London, 1928)

CARMAN, W.Y., *Jersey Militia Colours*, BSJ 1971 (Jersey, 1971)

Channel Islands Occupation Society, *Channel Islands Occupation Review* (Published alternately in Jersey and Guernsey, 1972–)

CLARK, R., *Dédicace des Eglises*, RGS (London, Part I Summer, 1975: Part II Winter, 1975)

COLLAS, V., *The Bells of St Andrew's*, RGS (London, Winter, 1974)

COX-JOHNSON, A., *John Bacon R.A. 1740–1799*, St Marylebone Society Publication No. 4 (London, 1961)

COYSH, V., *The Vale Castle and Mount Crevelt*, RGS (London, Winter, 1963)

—, *Nineteenth Century Defences in the Channel Islands*, TSG 1968 (Guernsey, 1969)

CURTIS, S.C., *Some Historical and Architectural Notes on the Priory at Lihou*, TSG 1912 (Guernsey, 1913)

—, *The Church Plate of the Deanery of Guernsey*, TSG 1913 & 1917 (Guernsey, 1914 & 1918)

—, *The Church Plate of the Deanery of Jersey*, BSJ 1917 (Jersey, 1917)

—, *The Evolution of the Country Churches*, TSG 1919 (Guernsey, 1920)

—, *The Frescoes at the Castel Church and St Apolline*, TSG 1927 (Guernsey, 1928)

—, *Low-side Windows in Guernsey Churches*, TSG 1928 (Guernsey, 1929)

DAVID, J.M., *The Early History of the Hanois Lighthouse*, TSG 1960 (Guernsey, 1961)

DAVIES, W., *Fort Regent A History*, Published Privately (Jersey, 1971)

DE GARIS, M., *The Story of St Pierre du Bois Church*, (Guernsey, 1970)

DE LA CROIX, J.N.R., *Jersey: Ses Antiquités, Ses Institutions, Son Histoire*, C. Le Feuvre (Jersey, 1859–61)

DE SAUSMAREZ, R., *The Court House of Fief Sausmarez at St. Martin's, Guernsey*, TSG 1959 (Guernsey, 1960)

DE SAUSMAREZ, R., & GIRARD, P., *James St. Vincent Saumarez Fourth Baron de Saumarez and his Estate in Guernsey*, TSG 1972 (Guernsey, 1973)

EWEN, A.H., *Essex Castle and the Chamberlain Family*, TSG 1957 (Guernsey, 1958)

EWEN, A.H., & de CARTERET, A.R., *The Fief of Sark*, The Guernsey Press Co. Ltd. (Guernsey, 1969)

GINNS, M., & BRYANS, P., *German Fortifications in Jersey*, W.M. Ginns & P.J. Bryans (Jersey, 1975)

Guernsey Society, *The Guernsey Farmhouse*, printed for the society by Thomas de la Rue & Co. Ltd. (London, 1963)

HANCOCK, J.R., *Some Notes on the History of the Parish Church of S. Michel du Valle*, (Guernsey, n.d.)

HARES, W.R.F., *A Pictorial Guide to the Parish Church, St Peter Port, Guernsey, C.I.* (Guernsey, n.d.)

JEE, N., *The Frescoes of the Castel Church*, RGS (London, Summer, 1962)

JOHNSTON, D.E., *Archaeology Study of the Nunnery*, ASQB (December, 1971)

KELLETT-SMITH, S.K., *The Obelisk on Herm*, RGS (London, Autumn, 1961)

KENDRICK, T.D., & HAWKES, A., *The Archaeology of the Channel Islands*, Methuen & Co. Ltd., London Vol. I. The Bailiwick of Guernsey (Kendrick), 1928, and Vol. II. The Bailiwick of Jersey (Hawkes), 1939

KNOCKER, G.S., *Freemasonry in Jersey*, M.F. Robinson & Co. Ltd., The Library Press (Lowestoft, 1930)

—, *The Windmills of Jersey*, BSJ 1936 (Jersey, 1936)

LANGTON, C., *The Seigneurs and Manor of Longueville*, BSJ 1930 (Jersey, 1930)

LECLUZE, M., *Une Eglise du XXe Siècle*, La Revue Française, Supplement to No. 182 (Paris, November, 1965)

LEE, G.E., *The Castel Church*, TSG 1904 (Guernsey, 1905)

LE GALLEZ, M.M., *Sainte Marie de Castro*, Guernsey Life (Guernsey, June, 1968)

LEGOUIX, S.Y., *John Cheere's Statue of George II*, The Connoisseur (London, April, 1975)

LE LIÈVRE, M., *Histoire du Méthodisme dans les Iles de la Manche 1784–1884*, Libraire Evangélique and Theophilus Woolmer (Paris and London, 1885)

LE MAISTRE, F., *The Great Whale of St Ouen and Notes Concerning Philippe Pirouet and Jean L'Escaudey*, BSJ 1977 (Jersey, 1977)

LEMPRIÈRE, R., *T.B. Davis – Benefactor*, BSJ 1968 (Jersey, 1968)

—, *History of the Channel Islands*, Robert Hale, (London, 1974)

—, *Portrait of the Channel Islands*, Robert Hale, (London, 1979)

LE PATOUREL, J., *Guernsey, Jersey and their Environment in the Middle Ages*, TSG 1974 (Guernsey, 1975)

LE PATOUREL, J. & J., *Lihou Priory: Excavations 1952*, TSG 1952 (Guernsey, 1953)

LITTLE, B., *St Peter Port Its Story and Its Buildings*, The National Trust of Guernsey (Guernsey, 1966)

MARETT, J.M., *The Old Town of St Aubin*, BSJ 1949 (Jersey, 1949)

MARSHALL, M., *Herm Its Mysteries and its Charm*, The Guernsey Press Co. Ltd. (Guernsey, 1974)

MAYNE, R.H., *Old Channel Islands Silver – Its Makers and Marks*, Print Holdings and Investments Ltd., (Jersey, 1969)

MESSAGER, J.L., *The Story and Description of St Thomas' Catholic Church, St Helier, Jersey, Channel Isles*, The British Publishing Co. Ltd., (Gloucester n.d.)

MOORE, R.D., *Methodism in the Channel Islands*, The Epworth Press (London, 1952)

MORLEY, G.R., *The Story of Methodism at St Aubin, Jersey*, Privately printed (Jersey, 1967)

MOULLIN, E.B., *Notes on the Registers of St Saviour's Parish, 1582–1693*, TSG 1953 (Guernsey, 1954)

—, *Domestic Architecture in Guernsey Before 1750*, TSG 1956 (Guernsey, 1957)

—, *Notes on the Registers of St Andrew's Parish*, 1578–1700, TSG 1952 (Guernsey, 1953)

MOURANT, A.E., *The Use of Ecréhous Stone in Jersey*, BSJ 1956 (Jersey, 1956)

NICOLLE, E.T., *Les Colombiers de Jersey*, BSJ 1928 (Jersey, 1928)

—, *Mont Orgueil Castle: Its History and Description*, The Beresford Library (Jersey, 1921)

O'NEIL, B.H.ST.J., *Castle Cornet Guernsey*, The States Ancient Monuments Committee (Guernsey, 1974)

PARTRIDGE, C., *Hitler's Atlantic Wall*, D.I. Publications (Guernsey, 1976)

PAYNE, R.W.J., *List of Memorials in the Parish Church of St Peter Port*, TSG 1966 (Guernsey, 1967)

POCOCK, H.R.S., *Jersey's Martello Towers*, BSJ 1971 (Jersey, 1971)

PRIAULX, T.F., *A Commemoration Medal of 1863*, RGS (London, Summer, 1955)

—, *The Story of the Church and Parish of St Saviour*, (Guernsey, 1969)

ROBINSON, G.W.S., *Guernsey*, David & Charles (Newton Abbot, 1977)

ROUSE, E.C., *Conservation of the Vault Paintings in the Jerusalem Chapel of La Hougue Bie, Jersey*, BSJ 1974 (Jersey, 1974)

RYBOT, N.V.L., *Grosnez Castle*, BSJ 1926 (Jersey, 1926)

RYBOT, N.V.L., *Heralrdy in the Channel Islands* Parts I, II & III, BSJ 1928 (Jersey, 1928); Part IV, TSG 1928 (Guernsey, 1929)

—, *Les Ecréhous. A Report on the Expedition of 1928 to the Islet which is called The Maître Ile*, BSJ 1933 (Jersey, 1933)

—, *The Islet of St Helier and Elizabeth Castle, Jersey*, States of Jersey, (Jersey, 1947)

—, *Gorey Castle*, States of Jersey (Jersey, 1978)

—, *Some Primitive Sculptures of the Channel Islands*, TSG 1930 (Guernsey, 1931)

SHARPE, F., *The Church Bells of Guernsey, Alderney and Sark*, Smart and Co. (Brackley, 1964)

SHAW, P.H., *The Parish Church of St Anne, Alderney*, (Alderney, n.d.)

SHAW, R., *Guide to the Parish Church of Ste Marguerite de la Forêt, Guernsey*, (Guernsey, n.d.)

SOHIER, H.W., *Jersey Justice with a Biographical Sketch*, Published Privately (Plymouth, n.d.)

States of Guernsey, *Billet d'Etat – Wednesday 27th February, 1974*, (Guernsey, 1974)

STEVENS, C.G., & ORS., *The Roman Pillar in St Lawrence's Church, Jersey; a Stocktaking*, BSJ 1975, (Jersey, 1975)

STEVENS, J., *Jersey in Granite*, The Royal Trust Company of Canada (C.I.) Ltd., (Jersey, 1977)

—, *Old Jersey Houses*, Published privately (Jersey, 1965):

—, *Old Jersey Houses Volume II*, Phillimore & Co. Ltd. (London and Chichester, 1977)

—, *A Short History of Les Augrès Manor, Jersey*, Jersey Wildlife Preservation Trust (Jersey, 1978)

STEVENS, J., & ARTHUR, J., *The Parish Church of Saint Mary, Jersey*, Rector and Church Officers of St Mary's Parish Church (Jersey, 1979)

SUTCLIFFE, S., *Martello Towers*, David & Charles (Newton Abbot, 1972)

THOMAS, E.M., & MOULLIN, J.E., *The Church at Cobo*, RGS (London, Winter, 1977)

TINGAY, J., *Catalogue of the 1978 Channel Islands Silver Exhibition*, Rotary Club of Guernsey (Guernsey, 1978)

THE PILOT, *Our Ancient Churches*, A Series of Articles in Vols. I – III (Jersey, 1946–49)

WARTON, R.G., *The Parish Churches of Jersey*, Société Jersiaise (Jersey, 1920)

W.,B.D., *Castle Cornet*, Jarrold & Sons Ltd., (Norwich, 1977)

WILLEY, F.J., *Halkett House*, BSJ 1963 (Jersey, 1963)

WINCKWORTH, J., *The Alderney Watermill*, ASQB (Alderney, March 1971)

WOOD, J., *Herm Our Island Home*, Robert Hale (London, 1972)

WOOLMER, S.C., & ARKWRIGHT, C.H., *Pewter of the Channel Islands*, John Bartholomew (Edinburgh, 1973)

Index

Index

The following abbreviations are used in the Index: A = Alderney; G = Guernsey; J = Jersey.

198